For Polly,

It's been such a
pleasure to know
you for so years!

Love
Pat

"The author takes readers by the hand and walks them through a treacherous territory."

—*Joan Marler, Founder and director of*
The Institute of Archaeomythology

"Rich, suggestive and courageous, the book nearly exploded in my hands. It is loaded with so much: with the author's own journey and the war going on among archaeologists over the goddess. She writes about both with passion and insight, not falling into the trap of romanticizing females as more benevolent than we are.

—*Anne Barstow, religious historian and*
author of Witchcraze *and* Joan of Arc

"This is an eye-opening and intimate journey through the eyes and heart of a cultural anthropologist passionately involved in uncovering the truth about the role of the goddess and gender equality in ancient civilizations — amid the assertions by so many (male) anthropologists that gender equality never really existed, despite so much evidence to the contrary. I loved it."

—*Anne Greenblatt, President of the*
Village Network of Petaluma

"This book has captured the new wave to create a modern-day village brilliantly and succinctly."

—*Charles R. Durrett, architect, and co-author with*
Kathryn McCamant of Creating Cohousing: Building
Sustainable Communities, *called the "bible" of the*
cohousing movement by The New York Times

"Interesting and powerful story of self-discovery through learning about history. I learned a lot!"

—*Chelan Schreifels, civil engineer*

Cover painting: Coastal California by Janet McBroom Johnson

Cover and page design by Anna Myers Sabatini

McBroom, Patricia.
Dance of the deities : searching for our once and future egalitarian society / Patricia McBroom.
Housatonic, Massachusetts : Green Fire Press, [2020]
©2020
164 pages : 1 illustration
9781732841451 (ISBN) 1732841454 (ISBN)
2020911214 (Library of Congress control number)
Includes bibliographical references (pages [155]-164).
1. Feminist theory. 2. Femininity (Philosophy) 3. Religion, Prehistoric.
4. Goddesses, Prehistoric. 5. Women. 6. Feminist anthropology.
7. Equality. 8. Patriarchy. 9. McBroom, Patricia.
HQ1190 .M33 2020
305.42 (23rd ed.)

Green
Fire
Press

Green Fire Press
PO Box 377 Housatonic MA 01236

DANCE OF THE DEITIES

SEARCHING FOR OUR ONCE AND FUTURE EGALITARIAN SOCIETY

PATRICIA MCBROOM

GREEN FIRE PRESS | HOUSATONIC, MASSACHUSETTS

Courtship of Inanna and Dumuzi: a sacred union, from
Mesopotamian clay plaque, probably 2000–1,600 BCE

DANCE OF THE DEITIES

To my beloved sister, Janet.

CONTENTS

PROLOGUE

MEETING THE EARTH SPIRIT

From a cramped, anxious curl, I turned over and opened up into a spread-eagled position on the mattress, with my arms flung wide on either side, letting the spirits of the plant medicine take over. It felt so good to relax into the floor, accepting and embracing the world.

This was no ordinary night. Two days earlier, I had seen Donald Trump elected president of the United States and I was still in a state of shock. Fortunately, I had already scheduled a medicine journey with psychedelic mushrooms and I was eager, though nervous, to find out what my brain would create under such conditions.

I'd been experimenting with psychedelics for about three years at the time, picking up an intention delayed for half a century. As a science writer in Washington, DC, in the late 1960s, I wrote about the transformative, spiritual experiments going on at Harvard University with LSD and psilocybin. I wanted to try psychedelics at the time, but lacked the support or access to take such a risk. So I waited. With the recent resurrection of circles using such medicines in northern California where I now live, I had the chance to attain the old ambition. In the intervening years, I had explored the physical world; now, after eighty years on Earth, it felt right to take an equally adventurous journey through my psyche.

My mind began to soar. The vaulted wooden ceiling above me darkened as night arrived—the only light coming from a circle of candles, the sacred circle where we had stated our intentions and ate the small, dry mushrooms. There were five of us, lying prone on mattresses on the floor with masks over our eyes, the better to experience internal space.

I took the mask off. I wanted to see the ceiling where a small, painted angel dangled from the rafters. I felt exhilarated, powerful, indefatigable. The fingers of my open hands seemed to gain enormous sensitivity, as if they could receive—and touch—everything. My arms embraced all children. I had become some sort of Earth spirit, a female spirit like the Great Goddess of antiquity—Gaia.

Now the energy was pouring through my body and mind and into the room. I thought of the recent election, in which Hillary Clinton lost the presidency, and I felt power as I had never felt it before. We did not lose. I knew that. We will never lose. I knew that too. Our spirit is triumphant. It can never be defeated. And by "we" I meant the Earth divinity as symbolized by the female. Ancient peoples worshipped such a divinity for 25,000 years before it was forcibly suppressed by the male-centered Abrahamic religions 3,500 years ago.

My left arm rose from the mattress and bent across my body as though I were holding a shield. It was a warning, a strike, to those who would violate me. My right arm remained outstretched, my hand with palm open, offering love and support. Both worked together: protection and receptivity.

Meanwhile, another part of my mind questioned my actions, as though I were performing a role. To ground myself, I held the ceremonial stick I had decorated earlier in the day to my chest. Fortunately, I was too carried away to be stopped by self-consciousness. Do and be what you are, I thought. Do not censure. Let it be. It feels so good.

My left arm fell back on the mattress and for a moment, I became another creature—a spider or a bug. It didn't matter what or who. Everything was of the Earth.

At this point, my guide came over to kneel beside me and ask how I was doing. He knew how much I had grieved in earlier trips with the earth medicine and he wanted to be sure I was okay. I rolled over.

"I am wonderful," I said.

"Good, I thought so," he replied, and went away again.

I didn't need any help of any sort. I was complete. Never had I *been so free of neediness, except in the arms of a lover. But even there, another person had been necessary.*

It seemed as if no time passed while I lay in this state of consciousness. Yet it had been three hours since our ceremony. Our guides were waking us up. I did not want to come back, was not ready to engage with language. The last thing I wanted to do was talk about this trip, though I had already begun to return to my body.

It was a strange feeling, to inhabit my body again. I could feel my arms and shoulders, chest and hips twitch as my normal human self came home. This self felt smaller, more earthbound, more ordinary.

But who had I been? What was this huge ego that had taken over? Did I really step into a divine spirit or was I experiencing some immature version of myself, which had never grown up?

My trip occurred at the same time that millions of women and men organized in the streets around the world to protest the Trump election and I do believe I was sharing some sort of global consciousness. Nevertheless, I was stunned by the archetype that arose. Never had I experienced such a personal taste of goddess power. The closest I had come was the sense of divine presence under a full moon thirty years earlier and that was without any chemical. It was also a solitary experience.

This time, I joined millions rising in protest against this parody of a patriarchy that had overtaken our country. Perhaps the only difference between us was that I had taken a plant of the earth that split my mind open to sacred experience, an experience that said NO, THIS MUST NOT STAND! and YES, I AM EARTH; I WILL CARE FOR YOU.

From that time forward, I decided to write a memoir of my search for equality and the sacred female, a search that has lasted off and on for fifty years, through my career as a science journalist and anthropologist.

There are many ways to conceptualize Gaia, an Earth spirit. Some practice rituals that recreate ancient pagan beliefs. Others find an avenue in believing that our western male God has no gender or was reformed by the feminizing influence of Jesus Christ, whose message of love humanized a rather brutal deity of the Hebrew Bible. For quite a few people, religion or spiritual belief of any kind is a nonstarter. They don't want any god or goddess. Science is enough.

But for me it has been essential to recover the cultural history of the sacred female because I need to safely internalize the sense of power and authority that comes from knowing there WAS a Goddess. She DID get suppressed. God, identified as HE, is NOT enough. Female divinity is missing in western monotheism and that will always be true.

References to a sacred female often raise the threat of out-sized mother power—a power that can trigger deeply embedded fear and opposition in those who have been badly mothered. The level of emotion generated around this idea reminds us that men and women both can have rather hateful memories of female power and wish never to see its face.

I've taken a long journey to owning the Goddess without fear—fear of being ridiculed for making outlandish claims, fear of exercising so much power that men would reject me, fear of violating a mountain of patriarchal thinking, fear of the darkness attributed to the sacred female, fear of the unknown, rejected, weak, maligned, dimly imagined face of a female creator.

I don't actually believe in a personified deity, whether male or female, and that may seem paradoxical considering the mental state I entered that night in 2016. But coming to understand the prehistoric goddess, however dimly, has brought her alive as an archetype in my brain. And it feels wonderful. I don't need a literal belief, but I do need to work through all the barriers that western patriarchy has raised against this sacred female.

I need to know that I—and all men and women—can hold a sacred image of the female without appearing to be crazy, frivolous or dangerous—off-balance in some way; that to exalt the mother does not diminish the father, that goddesses do not castrate men, that people once lived in harmony with such beliefs in the thousands of years before patriarchy.

Our minds often fall into opposing camps by thinking that if there had been a female divine, she must have been all powerful, like the Christian and Islamic male gods we are familiar with. But the evidence suggests that many, if not most, prehistoric people worshipped dual male and female gods. They had BOTH. Unlike modern humans, they did not argue over whether the divine spirit was male or female. A goddess was prominent, but she was not the only one.

At times, and in some cultures, there was an overarching female goddess. That was true during the early development of language in Mesopotamia, where Inanna became very nearly a monotheistic figure. This memoir will take you back to that period of early history as I resurrect the memory of Inanna in considering the terrifying aspects of a true nature goddess.

Most of my story, however, will delve into prehistory— the time before writing when archaeologists have only objects to interpret, without a recognizable language to direct those interpretations. I will take you on a journey into the deep past, 12,000 years ago, when human beings, at the beginning of the Agricultural Revolution, erected the first construction to endure through the centuries. It was not a house; it was a temple called Göbekli Tepe in what is now southeastern Turkey. The mysterious remains offer a Rorschach test for modern observers.

Similarly, other objects that survived into modern times from the Neolithic (period of the Agricultural Revolution) have generated multiple interpretations, marked by intense, often hostile, debate.

An enormous trove of figurines representing the female body, dug from the ground in Europe, gave rise to the extensive work of archaeologist Marija Gimbutas. For years, the male-dominated field of experts called these artifacts "Venus figures." Using the same and other objects, Gimbutas re-envisioned the entire European Era and its remains as the "Civilization of the Goddess," the title of one of her many books. Gimbutas galvanized a huge following, her work dominating European prehistory through the 1990s, giving new authority to many feminist scholars of religion.

A backlash began at the turn of the twenty-first century. One after another, archaeologists from the still male-dominated field began to deconstruct Gimbutas's work, until now it is no longer even offered to students. The notion of a prehistoric goddess draws snorts of derision. I will take you inside this backlash demonstrating the extent to which gender dominates interpretation. All of us, experts and nonexperts alike, have fallen victim to an image of the past created in the likeness of men alone. We see fighting, hunting and toolmaking as the drivers of human evolution. Rarely do we see the roles of women in that process.

The same male perspective resides in our story of genetic evolution during long years of change from nonhuman primates to modern humans. It's common to believe that men have always been dominant (for various reasons, often physical strength). I will show how that is not true. From my studies in physical and cultural evolution, I have discovered that gender equality has been a harbinger of our species. We have governed together, both in the metaphysical world and in our everyday lives.

As I talked about this memoir to a close friend of mine, he wanted to know if there had ever been a peaceful egalitarian society in the history of humankind. He suffered from notions of male aggression—his aggression—fearing that it was inborn through evolution. This is such a common source of misery—to think we humans can't live together in peace because our genes won't allow it. What else are we supposed to think, coming from a century with two world wars and weapons that could destroy the earth in a flash?

Because so much of anthropology has been written by men, it suffers from an overemphasis on aggression, warfare and hierarchy. Archaeology in particular delights in discovering monuments, palaces and rich burials—the impressive, beautiful remnants of the past. The field has little understanding of gender or social equality. So, it is all the more important to remember what we do know:

1. In equal cultures, gender is not a particularly important construct. Men and woman do similar things. Androgyny thrives.

2. Belief in a goddess or female founder almost always accompanies cultural authority held by women in that society.

3. Men are not naturally violent; culture makes them so for the purpose of using them in warfare.

This chronicle of my lifelong search for gender equality will be based on verifiable evidence. I aim to present a persuasive argument that female authority—joined with male authority—creates more democratic societies than we have known for the past 5,000 years of patriarchy.

I use my personal story as a lens through which you, the reader, can see the origin stories that experts have created about human evolution. Details of my personal life mix with scholarly material to deliberately create a subjective narrative. The approach highlights the fact that all such stories found in the academy have been written from a gendered perspective—a point of view that emphasizes the lives of men while ignoring those of women. Although new, more egalitarian stories are being told now, there is much work to be done. We need to rebuild evolution's House of Knowledge with two pillars holding up the roof, not one. In this research memoir I hope to lay one more brick on that foundation.

Much of the energy behind this memoir comes from a lifetime spent in the quest for an existential meaning in life. As I was growing into adulthood tragedy scarred me, raising questions about God and existence that I had no capacity to answer. My parents couldn't help; their own pain was too great. Teachers at the time were too insensitive. As a consequence, I was left alone at puberty in a way that set my course for life—away from the classic future for a woman of the 1950s and into a life of the mind. I wanted basic answers about why I was alive. And I wanted a voice.

ONE

GOD DIES; EVOLUTION ARRIVES

Ah, love, let us be true
To one another! for the world, which seems
To lie before us like a land of dreams,
So various, so beautiful, so new,
Hath really neither joy, nor love, nor light,
Nor certitude, nor peace, nor help for pain;
And we are here as on a darkling plain
Swept with confused alarms of struggle and flight,
Where ignorant armies clash by night.

— Matthew Arnold, "Dover Beach"

My world exploded in 1950, when I was 13. Everything I knew and counted upon disappeared and I was left on a "darkling plain," without a functioning family. My younger sister Barbara was dead at the age of ten, suddenly and without explanation taken from us by a mysterious disease. Her decline lasted only two months—a second in time that changed the rest of my life. I had watched over Barbara, taught her how to bicycle, helped her with math, defended her when she was threatened. When my parents seemed preoccupied with my older sister, I would retreat into a separate world of two—Barbara and me. It was enough.

One night she complained of pain in her lower stomach and, in the next moment, it seemed, she was lying in bed wasting away, her thin body getting so much thinner, covered in bed sores. We shared a bedroom and she moaned at night. I remember speaking out loud with irritation. "Oh, Barbara, can't you be quiet?" I hate that memory.

Then I remember that I also carried her up and down the stairs, day after day with loving care, so perhaps I should forgive myself.

None of the five physicians on the case could diagnose her illness. Various guesses at the time included an autoimmune disease and allergic reactions to new sulfa drugs. The final cause of death came with a heart attack, leaving us with a lifelong mystery; my mother would not permit an autopsy.

Some families come together after such a shock. My family disintegrated, in large measure because my mother, its powerful female center, collapsed into a pit of darkness so deep that recovery was impossible for a long time.

"I wanted to die," she told me years later when I finally could ask her why she hadn't been able to care about me.

My memories from that time are frozen into two scarring images.

The first is sitting beside the couch where my mother lay silent and tearless, holding her hand, talking to her about God, making up Sunday school stories about His Plan. The words became like dust in my mouth. But I kept it up because she seemed to brighten with my nurturance, and I could connect with her in the only way possible. Even with my 13-year-old brain, I knew she was suffering from the memories, not only of Barbara, but of her own mother's death when she was ten. I didn't blame her for her grief.

The second image is wandering in the fields around our house, screaming in my mind at the sky, where I supposed God lived. It was inconceivable to me that God would leave me so alone. "What kind of God are you? How can you do this to me?" There was no salvation—no hope—no comfort—no explanation—certainly no sign of heavenly existence. When I prayed to the ceiling at night, lying next to Barbara's empty bed, there was nothing.

My father was in despair—and he was a drinker. My older sister, Janet, with whom I didn't get along at the time, took refuge in her teenaged friendship circle. Two years later, when I was 15, we moved from Sacramento to Pasadena, so community was gone as well. Nothing was left.

In the years that followed, I have few if any memories except for excruciating loneliness and the paradoxical pleasures of a maturing young body. Within a year of Barbara's death, I was transformed from a pudgy kid with braces on her teeth, to a thin, sexy young woman aware that, at least in body, I could find connection. But the world, whether practical or spiritual, didn't make much sense to me. As I began adult life, I was driven by the need to answer the Big Questions.

Albert Camus' novel, *The Stranger*, was my guiding theme: Human beings create our own meaning in the absence of God; we must act. So I had purpose. But beneath the drive to rationally understand the world lay a thick layer of emotional pain.

CHILDHOOD

The break from childhood was perhaps more radical for me than for most white children born and raised in northern California. We had a sweet life living in a community surrounded by open fields on the eastern edge of Sacramento. I was shy and in love with school. I earned straight As and loved nothing more than shooting my hand into the air in answer to some word quiz. But put me in front of an audience where I had to perform—pure misery. I joined the band in grade school. I had no musical talent and ended up on the bells where I had nothing to do except hit one note during an entire composition. I remember sitting there with the stick in my hands ready to strike. The music droned on; my anxiety went off the scales. The moment came—and passed. I sat there with the stick in my frozen fingers. I had missed the moment!

I partially recovered self-respect when I was chosen to be the valedictorian of our graduating class. I will never forget the bright white lights shining in my face as I repeated by rote memory the words I had written. It wasn't a great moment, but at least I didn't freeze.

My summers as a child were memorable. The mountains were only two hours from our home and we camped out often near the crystal-clear waters of Lake Tahoe, where you could see your toes on the sandy bottom. I loved the granite range of the majestic Sierra Nevadas so much that I interpreted the wind rustling in its pine trees as the voice of God.

Further north lay some really wild territory. I remember my father shining his flashlight at the constellations in the Milky Way that glittered overhead. One night our campground was invaded by a herd of wild horses and he was out there in the night flailing his arms to drive them away from our tents.

Families in our community were highly connected, even building a Congregational church together. My mother and father helped design the buildings; Janet was part of a teen-aged network that inaugurated the first youth group (they were bonded enough that some members of that group continued to meet at Lake Tahoe until just a few years ago.) During the World War II years, I would wheel my little red wagon down the winding country roads collecting newspapers for the war effort. One day, Janet, already recognized by our family as an artist—a calling she would follow for life—painted the face of Tojo, the Japanese prime minister, on a telephone pole after which we all threw rotten tomatoes at it. What a kick!

Part of my shyness arose from birth order. I was the middle child in a three-girl household, which meant I was left mostly alone while my parents focused on my sisters. My older sister, Janet, garnered most of their attention, while I forged a close relationship with my younger sister, Barbara. The excessive attention was not so good for Janet, and I would watch her emotional exchanges with our parents from the edge of the doorway, knowing even then that I was the lucky one, if overlooked.

My father—a sweet, short Irishman given to love of the bottle—was a most intelligent man, bright enough to go from a farm in Wyoming to MIT for a degree in civil engineering. That career choice kept him employed throughout the Great

Depression building bridges for the state of California.

My heart melts as I remember him wrestling with us on the grass with laughing delight or telling us stories night after night at the dinner table—about his own past, about history, about astronomy, about whatever. I don't know where he got all his stories, but he told them with relish and we were mesmerized. When I was little, he would hold Barbara and myself in his arms while he read *The Rhyme of the Ancient Mariner* to us: "Water, water everywhere and not a drop to drink." Unforgettable.

And there are more painful memories—a sense that he was not equal to my mother, an awareness of trouble beneath the "totally normal" 1940s household, where father left for work each morning in hat and suit to earn all the money, while mother stayed home to raise the children, iron, wash, clean and can fruit—isolated, bored and depressed.

For a middle-class family, we lived in rather upscale surroundings, with a big two-story house surrounded by an acre of lawn, plus a tennis court, which my father built at night after work, apparently trying to satisfy my mother's desire to elevate our status in the community. I don't know where that idea came from, but it informs a painful memory of Dad sitting at the table late one night, exhausted from his labors. Tears escaped from his eyes, not a common sight. I felt such pain for his sorrow and loneliness. I was just a young kid—I could not help him, but the empathy I felt at that moment imbedded this image in my mind for the rest of my life, along with sorrow for him and anger at my mother for "making" him build such a thing.

She had power. There were no two ways about that. Power over us and power with him. We didn't see much outright fighting, but silence told volumes. And I could see that he would rather retreat than confront her. She had some kind of unshakable, unbendable authority that everyone in my family understood. I remember thinking long ago, "Why do I need God? I have Mom." When I expressed that thought recently to my nephew, Erik, he laughed with knowing awareness. No explanation needed.

She once told me a story about going outside her house during a huge windstorm and howling with the wind. She became it. Imagine, this straight-laced Presbyterian woman who used to point out every flaw my sister and I had—like a slip showing beneath the skirt—becoming a wild woman, throwing up her arms and howling as the wind howled around her. I love that image. It is her, indomitable.

I couldn't get the best of her—ever. Not until she was more than 100 years old did she break down and cry, asking Janet and me for forgiveness for things we had tried over decades to discuss with her. I loved her. I loved her. I wish I had held her in my arms at the end instead of asking like a little child, after she gave me instructions for her death, "What shall I do then, Mom?" She answered, "I don't know Pat. I'm tired." She died that night.

YOUNG ADULTHOOD

Power, nurturance and safety—all these words inform my memories of mother. She was absolutely reliable in a crisis. Highly intelligent, she had some sort of solid connection with reality and a passion for gardening. In another era, she might have been a botanist.

To me, her word was Law—not always a positive experience for a child. Along with the safety and reliability came darker aspects: dominance, anger and fear. Mom's disapproval—the scowling signs of anger—could put me into a twist and I would retreat from whatever willfulness I was on the verge of expressing. Being sent to my room was comparable to descending into purgatory. I could cry with such outrageous abandon that she finally couldn't stand it and had to release me. That got to be a pattern.

I also experienced the dark side of female power from Janet, who could scare the daylights out of me when she got mad and chased me around the dining room table or threatened to hit me, which seemed to happen often. When I would run to my mother for protection, she would punish Janet and the whole thing would be set up for another round of the same dynamic. In adulthood, Janet has given me precious compassion and support in times that I needed help, so we have long since healed these childhood memories. We share a marvelous love; there is no one I care more about than her and I know that care is returned.

But these early dysfunctional aspects of my family gave me a good dose of female aggression that became part of my own psyche, bringing lifelong awareness that we women can be as dark and destructive as men are in contemporary society, though its expression manifests differently. I struggled for years with my feminine psyche. Was I too dominant? How many ways could I give my power away to a romantic partner? What does femininity mean anyway in white American society? No matter, I didn't match up. I wasn't a woman in some fundamental way, though I loved men to pieces.

I know I am not alone in these reflections. So many women have had to create new gender identities in the past century in our quest to end patriarchy and achieve equality. Our stories are the same and also different. For me, the journey began with a complete aversion to the life of a post-war California suburban woman. I was NOT going to be a wife whose career was "Mrs." I wanted a man to be my partner, but only with equality. I wanted to see the world, have a voice, make my mark—and then I would get married and have children, I thought.

The major impetus for my leap into the wide, wide world was a trip to India in 1959. I was among fourteen students at the University of California chosen to represent America in a three-month goodwill visit to what was at the time a new democracy. That trip opened my eyes to a world of unimaginable color, variety, activity, beauty and human suffering; to a world of involvement and complexity. I never looked back. Many who were selected for Project India—a yearly pre-Peace Corps venture that lasted from 1952 to 1964—felt their lives changed by the experience. I was one of them. When I returned to California, it seemed grey and unexciting, with cement freeways everywhere and boring suburbs.

I took a temporary job as secretary to the dean of women students at UCLA while I figured out what to do with my life. Various career opportunities were offered on campus, including one from the National Security Agency, which would have gotten me to Washington, DC, one of my ambitions. But as I thought about it, I gazed across the quad at the School of Journalism and suddenly realized that I wanted to expose information, not hide it. My lasting purpose in life became apparent: I would make esoteric knowledge available to the public. And so it has been through the decades.

LEAVING HOME

I earned a master's degree in journalism in 1963, a time when jobs were plentiful—even for women. I had little awareness of the privilege men enjoyed in society. Of course, the want ads for men and women were separated and listed on different pages of the newspaper, but otherwise I thought male dominance was a thing of the past. How would I know? My family patterns resembled a matriarchy. I was quite ignorant of the world outside and Californians, in my experience then, rarely admitted to having prejudice of any kind, whether racial or gender-based.

Two years later, I was in Washington, DC looking for employment as a journalist. I had wanted a voice, an informed voice, and suddenly I was covering science in an entry level job as a reporter for the Science News Agency. It was a wonderful time to be a science writer, particularly on my beat, the social sciences. The field was new and women were welcomed because we had brains and didn't have to challenge male hegemony on the local police beat. Moreover, the public badly needed help in understanding the violence that was sweeping the country during the civil rights movement and anti-Vietnam war protests of the Lyndon Johnson era.

I delved with relish into sociology, psychology and anthropology, interviewing academics who were more than willing to expound on social violence. It was the opportunity they were waiting for to have some relevance outside academe. Of all these perspectives, the one I fell in love with was anthropology, particularly the story of human evolution. Broadly based on both biology and culture, anthropology included incredible female pioneers like Margaret Mead and Jane Goodall; nevertheless, the intellectual spine of the canon that told us who we were as human beings was written mostly by men based on studies of men. In the 1960s, the story was one of violence.

That narrative was exemplified by anthropologist Raymond Dart, the man who identified the first bipedal hominid artifact, an Australopithecine infant skull in South Africa. The so-called Taung child challenged preconceived ideas about human evolution because its brain was tiny. Dart had to survive years of isolation and defamation among British anthropologists for this notion that upright posture preceded brain growth. Perhaps that's why his message was so passionate. When I interviewed him, I remember him almost shouting, "We are killers!" with his white hair flying, it seemed, in all directions. (The evidence for his statement were the bashed-in skulls of other animals associated with Australopithecine remains, apparently its food source.)

That message came through dramatically at the beginning of the movie *2001: A Space Odyssey* when an ape evolving into human throws its club into the air. In the next frame, time moves forward millions of years and the club becomes a space ship. Then, as now, the story of human evolution was dominated by male-generated images of violence and technology, represented by a primate thumping the ground with the limb of some defeated opponent.

After speaking to Dart, I went back to the office and wrote his story with gusto. Considering the urban riots in the country at the time and our immoral war against the Vietnamese north, it seemed totally appropriate to accept the killer thesis. Sort of like whipping ourselves. Bad people! And nothing you could do about it, of course, since it was built into our genes through evolution. Later, the years I spent studying human evolution and culture in graduate school at the University of Pennsylvania brought me to a different conclusion: the story changes when the female voice is included.

As satisfying as my career became, at the same time my personal life sank into deep pain. Though sex was easy, I could not seem to establish a lasting relationship. Partners proliferated in the years of the sexual revolution, but I soon realized that for me physical intimacy did not lead to deeper intimacies. I got pregnant and obtained an abortion in a darkened doctor's office (before Roe v. Wade), refusing all but financial help from the man who made me pregnant. I could take care of it myself, I thought, and then I couldn't. I had to call him at the last moment to pick me up, which he willingly did. But I did not love him; we were not a match. I spent the next few days sobbing in the bathtub, wondering why this was so painful.

Then there was the man who took me to Paris and wanted to marry me. But I could not do that; I didn't love him. He left. The pain grew. I spent nights thinking about suicide.

One morning I woke up and heard the birds singing. I knew that I would never kill myself. The world was beautiful. I wanted to live.

TWO

CREATION OF A FEMINIST

It was 1970. I was living in downtown Philadelphia working as a science writer for the city's major newspaper, The Philadelphia Inquirer. *A knock came on the door. On the other side was a man who had come to live with me. He was also a science writer for the paper. We would live together for the next eight years, during which time my life course would change forever, taking a radical and unexpected new direction. At the time, I didn't think about whether it was advisable or not to hook up with my colleague at work. We were peers after all—no differences in authority. It should be all right, I thought.*

I went to the *Philadelphia Inquirer* in 1969 as a science writer, happy to be avoiding the usual destination for female journalists—the women's pages. The first woman in the news-room, covering a field that editors knew next to nothing about, I felt privileged. Nobody interfered with my work, though they did watch me carefully to see what I would do. I learned that I passed muster, I remember, the day I got a front-page story from a biology conference on the newly discovered anti-inflammatory effects of aspirin; the editors let me know I was doing the job. It was a good life, being a specialist, breaking ground.

And the paper was breaking ground. Nothing to speak of when I first got there, often called a "rag" that served the political interests of its owner, the *Inquirer* was soon bought out by the Knight Ridder chain and began to beef up its reporting staff. The new owners had decided to make this their flagship; they put money into it and it showed in the young, talented crew that soon arrived. We formed a cohort, distinct from the older guys who'd been there for years. Somebody dubbed them "the lemon grove" because they sat around with sour expressions, sneering at any new initiative. "We're second here, and we LIKE it," a member of the grove sneered at me one night about living in Philadelphia. He was referring to the city's classic standing compared to New York. But the revived newspaper had no intention of being second to anything and soon was publishing stories on entrenched political interests.

This being the early 1970s however, other energies were also arising, specifically the desire by writers to have more control over their work. Chafing at the autocratic power of publishers and wanting more influence, reporters in major cities around the East and Midwest began to publish what they called "journalism reviews"—small newsletters that criticized the way news was covered at their own papers.

Written by small groups of journalists in many cities—New York, Chicago, Baltimore, Philadelphia—these reviews held local editors and publishers up to public scrutiny and criticism. It was a heady experience to think you could criticize your boss in public without heavy reprisals, but, hey, these were revolutionary days. It didn't take long before the truth of corporate power landed.

Philadelphia's journalism review, which was read by the corporate owners of the *Inquirer* back in Akron, Ohio, had been established by the man I shared my life with, *Inquirer* science writer Donald Drake. We made our home together, while each of us covered a part of the science writing beat at work.

At night after work, Don would enthusiastically dig into writing, editing and publishing the review while I twiddled my thumbs on the sidelines. I had little or no interest in devoting my free time to putting out such a newsletter. Nor did I want to criticize my own newspaper. I just wanted to succeed at my day job; few women had such a good one, and exposing my editors in public was the last thing I wanted to do.

One night, while I relaxed in a warm bath, Don pleaded for my support.

"I need you to help me do this," he said.

I heard the appeal. "OK," I replied. "I'll stop complaining, but I'm not going to write any stories for you."

But many top journalists at the paper did contribute stories and each month, our editors were faced with criticism of decisions they made. Perhaps one month, the paper ran too many stories from the police department. The next month, perhaps, the editors spilled too much ink on protest demonstrations rather than covering the issues involved. That was a favorite complaint at science meetings, where the protests in the early 1970s were drowning out basic science news. Then there was the claim that writers on a newspaper should have the freedom to tell the truth they knew, rather than hold to a false objectivity or slant news to fit editorial directive.

Very soon, the mood upstairs at the *Philadelphia Inquirer* got rather ugly. Reporters writing the review began to tell Don they were getting pressure to quit this gig. They stopped quickly. It was too dangerous. Easy for them; not so easy for me.

I tried to separate myself from Don's activity. I went to the executive editor at the time, John McMullan, and told him I had nothing to do with the review, that it was purely Don's mission. He did not believe me. I remember that at some point, we just stared at each other, hostility rippling through the air. I left his office knowing that nothing I said would change his mind.

My cherished career at the paper went into a sinkhole. I was taken off science writing and put on obituaries. It was deadly. Don's punishment was a lengthy assignment in a mental hospital where, he surmised, he wouldn't find any news.

My time in purgatory lasted six months—a time of transformation that drove my life into a completely new path. I became a feminist, a change that has lasted a lifetime. From that time forward, I would find myself challenging patriarchy in whatever way possible. A small—or not so small—sign of that conversion is that I never wore a skirt again (other than some of those long filmy things popular in the 1990s).

I saw no reason why I had to suffer for Don's professional sins. I began to understand that rather than being seen as an individual, I was being seen as a female collaborator in this situation.

A note that I saw, sent from one editor to another, referred to me as "Drake and Company." I fumed at the knowledge that I did not even warrant a name. In this male-dominated environment, I had no power.

While my career was going into eclipse, other journalists and writers in the movement throughout the East and Midwest were brimming with enthusiasm. In New York, they held their first "counter convention," the A.J. Liebling convention, named after the famed *New Yorker* magazine writer who had advocated that journalists take a stand against their more right-wing publishers. A star-studded cast of speakers attended the convention, including *New York Daily News* columnist Jimmy Breslin, who urged us to "have a voice."

A "voice" was what I had set out in life to achieve, but at that juncture, at that convention, my voice was all but muted by the pain of reprisals. Worst of all, I couldn't claim that I had acted on any principle or that I had done anything to warrant punishment. I was just a woman who took the heat, a mere ghost who drifted through the rooms unable to utter my name. No name. This was my worst fate. Anything was better.

People may wonder why I did not enthusiastically endorse this writer's "rebellion." My rebellion was occurring at another level, against the destiny of women in that era—women who had little influence outside their homes. Just to succeed in the outside world, to navigate a male-dominated workplace, to find new, more equal, paths in personal life, to put my perspective into the established order—that was enough. Actually, the thought of bringing down the established order did not occur to me—until I returned from the A.J. Liebling convention.

My rebellion began upon returning to Philadelphia. With the logic of a child, or a martyr —not sure which fits better—I decided that I would commit the sin I was being punished for. I wrote a front-page article for the Philadelphia review titled "Tyranny in the Newsroom." The subject was a nasty, bloody fight between *Inquirer* management and the Newspaper Guild. And it really was nasty. The paper was out to break the union in a series of inhumane actions, such as firing a popular editor because he was close to retirement and they could save money by letting him go early. The Guild was up in arms. I wrote that story and was fired the day it was published, hours after I distributed it in person in the newsroom. You could say I was getting in their faces.

No surprise that I was fired. But I was shocked, or more accurately traumatized. You might think I knew what I was doing, but that would be wrong. Considering the emotions running through the newsroom at the time, one could imagine a groundswell of support for me. That did not happen. Friends fell away. The Guild's primary interest—hours and wages—did not include editorial policy. I was alone.

I tell this story with reluctance and chagrin. It is a painful but necessary memory to recount, because, as the saying goes, "Feminists are not born; they are made by life."

A few people acknowledged that I had taken the heat for my partner; most did not. I remember those individuals for their ability to see the larger gender issues at play, but I knew for the first time in my life that I needed to understand how society was structured; I needed to understand patriarchy. This was 1972. Nixon had been re-elected. The sixties were over.

Still living with Don, but now with a paltry freelance income, I could not help becoming dependent in a way I had determined would never happen to me. The role I dreaded, that of "wife," took over my life, bringing loss of prestige and personal power.

Doctors gave me tricyclic antidepressant meds to lift the lid of despair and calm the rage beneath it. Newly marketed, with more powerful side effects than such drugs today, they acted like cement in my nervous system. I think I did not achieve any alertness for three weeks until my body adapted and then I was no longer the person I remembered. Lonely and marginalized at home as a freelance writer, I watched Don and our friends prosper at the *Inquirer* under new management headed by Eugene Roberts from the *New York Times*.

I lived well enough in a grand three-story townhouse on 22nd St. in Philadelphia, but I was no longer financially equal with my partner and that cut into my self-esteem. And the resentment grew—resentment born of anger that Don had thrived at the *Inquirer* while I had lost my career. For several years, he did not acknowledge his role in my fate. Power shifted. I could feel the loss of equality and knew that I would have to leave him when I could get the resources to do so. Antidepressant pills no longer tamped down the anger. I imagined that a black tree, symbolizing my relationship with Don, was spreading its branches throughout my brain. He grew increasingly adept at managing my outbursts while gathering support from our friends at the *Inquirer*.

"You didn't have to write that article," an *Inquirer* friend said to me, as we were lifted over the waves of the Chesapeake Bay on the sailboat Don and I owned. "You could have waited out the punishment on the obituary desk and eventually your beat would have been reinstated."

Well, maybe, I thought. Perhaps men have been trained for generations in the hierarchy at work and they know how to submit when a boss goes after them. As a woman (and a feminist by this time), I never got such training.

But I did have an opportunity to function as a mother to Don's daughter Valerie, who had come to live with us when she was 16. After a fairly rocky start, when I got a full dose of teenaged anger, we arrived at a truce. "I'm the only daughter you will ever have," she said to me one day," a statement that has reverberated through me ever since. She was so right. I've loved her ever since.

Meanwhile, I won a contract from the National Institute of Mental Health (NIMH) to write a monograph on the genetics of behavior, bringing together all the research on mental health and intelligence that the Institute had supported to that time. I was happy to win the contract, but it was a monumental task to integrate such information.

I had also, by this time, entered a graduate program at the University of Pennsylvania's Department of Anthropology for the express purpose of understanding male dominance. Where did it come from in human society? Is it built into our genes? How does patriarchy work? Why does a gender hierarchy exist?

Completing graduate level courses while writing a monograph on genetics drove me nearly crazy. Periodically, I would find myself experiencing all the mental diseases I wrote about. Ah, schizophrenia! Spend two months writing about these symptoms and you will find them in yourself. Or, how about manic-depressive disease? I had that too!

The monograph, titled *Behavioral Genetics*, was published in 1980.[1] Forty scientists at NIMH vetted the manuscript, the first popular synthesis of the genetics underlying personality and IQ. My department awarded me a master's degree in physical anthropology for the chapter on genetic differences in intelligence.

Five years after losing my sweet career at the *Inquirer*, I was ready to leave Don, even though he had finally acknowledged that I had been his fall guy. Executive editor Roberts had told him that he had examined the records and had concluded that I was indeed scapegoated. I will always remember the night Don came home from work, walked in the kitchen and said, "You were right; you paid the price for me." The validation was sweet, but by that time it was not enough. I was well into my studies in anthropology and I was committed to finding some answers that would be relevant to all of us, men and women alike, who were struggling to achieve equality. My career as a newspaper reporter was over, as was my union with Don.

I began my search at the University by studying primate evolution, figuring that if male dominance was universal among human cultures, as many authorities claimed, it would be evident in the proto-human past, including among our cousins, the Great Apes. This was the grand story of human evolution that I originally fell in love with when I began science writing.

Within a few years at Penn, in the late 1970s, I found what I was looking for and more. I came to understand the origins of male dominance and I met the Great Goddess of prehistory.

THREE

ONE GREAT BIG MALE BABOON

It is 2014 and I have just had my first experience with a psyche-delic medicine, the sacred mushrooms whose effects are both amazing and unpredictable. I have no idea what visions will come. My studies in primate evolution have long been over; nevertheless, the old passion with our human story arises again. After a long period of silence and existential angst, I see this:

> *I have just come down out of the trees. I look out on the savannah as sunlight turns the grasslands a bright yellow. Standing beside me is my guide on the journey who looks like a quirky female. Our bodies are covered with a furry-like substance and she has a wisp of hair that falls over her eyes. We straighten up on our back feet to see better over the distance. Way off on the horizon, I see a city whose towers rise into the clouds. We stare for a long moment; then I turn to her and say, "Let's go back into the trees and eat fruit." We laugh.*

In my vision, I am a proto-human, a creature at the dawn of human evolution when the human line split from the chimpanzee's. We had very small brains at this point, but we were beginning to walk out of the forest onto the savannah where we would evolve into modern humans. That would take us five to seven million years—an unimaginably long time, during which we would learn to run, hunt down big game, triple the size of our brains, and most of all, develop complex culture.

What I am seeing in the distance is the end result of that evolution and it does not look good: immense cities, unending threats, ecological damage. Better that we don't evolve, is what I am thinking. But nostalgia for an Edenic past that does not threaten the earth and all humanity won't help. The only way through is to wise up and use our social consciousness far better than in the past. We can do it, but we probably won't. I am not optimistic.

When I started with primate behavior in the 1970s, there was no such thing as a female ape with any agency. The field was dominated by images of big male baboons with six-inch long fangs, mouths fully extended in a huge gapes that looked insanely violent.

They were a metaphor for aggressiveness and cunning. The males fought for access to females. The only time they displayed any interest in offspring was when one would snatch a baby baboon and hold it to its chest to deter attack by another male. They fit the paradigm at the time of *Man the Hunter*,[2] a primary text of human evolution based on the rise of big-game hunting. Tool use, social organization and a growing brain were supposedly the result of "man" learning to hunt large animals in groups.

The species that really stood out at the time was the Hamadryas baboon of Egypt, a sickening example of male dominance. This baboon, which has extreme sexual dimorphism (males twice the size of females), functioned by collecting females in groups and herding them around, biting any that strayed outside their prescribed territory. We called this a "harem" and it was another possible model for human evolution.

Baboons, however, shared fewer genes with humans than did the Great Apes, among whom male dominance was, at the time, less evident. Gorillas, yes. High sexual dimorphism but not particularly aggressive; families dominated by males. Chimpanzees, our closest relatives, appeared peaceful, not male-dominated, according to the early work done by Jane Goodall; her story changed in later years when she discovered group violence and killing among the chimpanzees at her Gombe Research Station in Tanzania.

Then there were the gibbons. Males and females, similar in size, mated for life, didn't fight much; lived in trees. We heard little about gibbons and nothing at all about bonobos, a species with a profound love of sex and little appetite for violence. Humans are genetically as closely related to bonobos as we are to other chimps.

Not all primatologists subscribed to the male aggression thesis. I remember fondly the work of Professor Robert Harding at Penn, who explored the evolution of fathering behavior in primates, showing its gradual appearance in monkeys, apes, hominids and modern humans. Sitting in his class was like waking up to humanity: *Oh yes, there we are.*

In coming to understand primate behavior, I also came to see that no one species could be a model for humans. Gender equality and peacefulness were as common as male dominance, just not often discussed.

I am not saying that male academics and intellectuals had bad intentions; only that their perceptions were constrained by gender. They were following an intellectual thread that had developed over a century of theory building when human evolution was viewed as the "study of man" or "mankind." No mention was made of the role of females in evolution except as recipients of male action.

A TEMPLE OF ANTHROPOLOGY

The stories we hear every day in the public arena about human nature come from such places as the University of Pennsylvania Museum and other top-flight centers of learning. This is where academics, based on their studies of a specific species or human group, generate new hypotheses about human behavior and feed it out to the larger society through scientific publications and eventually the press—hypotheses such as: "Man is a killer"; "Hunters had to organize to hunt big game; therefore male activities produced language"; "Stone toolmaking built the new human brain."

We would sit around food and coffee in the cafeteria—professors and students alike—talking about these stories, learning them, spinning them.

The cafeteria was located at the heart of the museum, on the second floor, between two wings, one devoted to classrooms and the other to various research functions such as deciphering cuneiform script from Mesopotamia. On either side of the room, huge floor to ceiling windows looked out on gardens. Beneath us on the first floor were museum spaces filled with Egyptian mummies and big stone stelae from the classic Mayan culture of Mesoamerica.

I thought I was going to school in a temple of anthropology. And I was. This is where we interpreted the signs of human evolution and behavior, where we made sense of an overpowering reality that, if ever fully comprehended, would strike us dumb.

But as critical as storytelling is to all the sciences, the lopsided emphasis on male dominance and aggressive primates like male baboons was intolerable. I learned that primate variability was immense. Each species brought its own behavioral storehouse; no one species represented humanity. I needed to move on. The real story of human evolution was hidden in creatures long gone—hominids that over millions of years evolved into Homo sapiens.

BECOMING HUMAN

Long after our hominid ancestors left the forest and began walking upright, their brains began a phenomenal growth trajectory, until, at the end, modern humans had three times the cranial capacity of other apes. Almost all of this growth was in the cerebral cortex, including frontal lobes—the locus of analysis, so-called "executive" ability and logic.

The cerebral cortex is wired, not to the outside world, but to other regions of the brain that do perceive the world. The older brain structures are shared by other primates; less so the cerebral cortex. The new "human" cortex lacks specific, identifiable functions, but it is known that it can act on sensory perception to inhibit signals, so that the reality we see is shaped by information already gathered. What we see and hear is a model of reality; each individual has his or her own version. In this way, we create our stories, built from a reality that each individual sees differently.

Professor Alan Mann taught physical anthropology and he was good. I remember that he did not resort to the usual explanation for brain expansion—hunting and tool use—arising from male activities. Instead he spoke of the birth of incredibly immature infants in social groups where families with sex roles emerged to support offspring who could not fend for themselves. It was the start of a new, profound understanding of the impact of bipedalism on females.

As the story has evolved since then, walking upright—not to mention running—narrowed the birth canal of hominid females, making birthing more difficult. Simply put, the pelvic channel was too narrow for a child's skull to pass through, with the result that babies had to be born prematurely. As brain evolution progressed, creating ever larger heads, the problem got worse. Ultimately, nature's solution was for females to give birth long before the fetus was fully developed, compared to other apes. Not only was a newborn hominid brain seriously immature, but the skull had to be so flexible that its plates could squeeze together in the birth canal, becoming fixed only after birth.

Rather than maturing in the womb, the hominid brain exploded in growth after birth, tripling in size in the early years of life, requiring whole new levels of social support and acquiring a plasticity that was unknown on Earth. Here was an animal that no longer acted upon instinct but learned how to live in the world in a culturally specific way. In large part, humans learn through environment so well because our neural wiring is so incomplete when we emerge into life.

A new and dramatic need for social groups—tribes—to care for the young emerged in human evolution, as well as ethnic and language boundaries. You might expect that this would be a time when women would finally be included in the story of humankind. After all, women were dominant in childrearing;

their language shaped the newborn brain; indeed, language could have evolved significantly this way, driven by interaction between mother and child. The notion of sacredness, the idea of goddesses and gods in the natural world could have arisen from the relationship between mother and child, born of the universal love in that union. Certainly, many of the social rules and customs would have been passed from women to children, forming their brains to accept the cultural expectations of a particular group. Indeed, women theorists did begin to tell such stories in the 1970s.

FEMALE VOICES

Those of us who hung out in the museum cafeteria took heart when we heard about "woman the gatherer," a thesis explored by Francis Dahlberg,[3] demonstrating in no uncertain terms that women provided most of the food in hunter-gatherer societies. Such peoples, (at least those that had been studied in the past two centuries by anthropologists and presumably in prehistoric times as well), were not sustained primarily by male hunters of big game but by women who foraged.

In the data Dahlberg edited, men provided an occasional feast of meat from hunting, but women collected sixty to eighty percent of the daily diet from plants and small animals. Here at last was a new and significant role for women, other than being traded as marriage collateral between patriarchal tribes. (I cannot forget the tender mercies of Claude Lévi-Strauss, the famed anthropologist whose theories reduced all women to the status of property to be exchanged among men of different tribes. If one wanted, as a woman, to feel like a piece of meat, this was a good place to start.)[4]

So if women provided the lions' share of the food in ethnographic studies, what did the men do all day? One thing they did was sit in the longhouse and talk about ancestors, keeping cultural mythologies alive.

Several years later, I learned from work by anthropologist Barbara Smuts[5] that baboon troops were organized by *female* hierarchies that passed power through birth, from top-ranked females to female offspring. Males moved in and out but were not resident in these groups, and, despite their big fangs, did not dominate the females that often chose their mates. Goodbye Hamadryas and harems. You will not be missed!

But androcentric bias in academic studies dies hard, particularly when the majority of current scholars are men, relying on male scholarship built into the culture over many years.

UNIVERSAL MALE DOMINANCE?

The most widely propagated notion about culture and gender in the 1970s was that male dominance is universal in human society. After all, we can look around ourselves in modern culture and see it everywhere, not just in repressive Middle Eastern cultures where women risk their lives by simply driving a car, but in Western culture as well where misogyny lurks in the hearts of men and women who may have no idea they discredit female power.

If it is so widespread in modern life, then logically it must be somehow built into the human race, if not by genes, then by physical strength. How about that one? Bigger animals get the food and the power, right? Well, not really. During the millions of years that hominids were building big brains, they also were systematically losing sexual dimorphism. That is, men and women were coming to resemble each other in height and weight, so that among some cultural groups, a difference between men and women is small or even nonexistent. On average, throughout the human race, men are about fifteen percent larger than women, though this difference varies greatly, depending on food, work, cultural habits and geography.

It was about this time that a female deity broke into my consciousness for the first time as something other than a kind of droll myth dressed in Grecian robes.

In 1978, Merlin Stone shook the field of religious studies with her book *When God was a Woman*,[6] providing in exquisite detail the multiple ways ancient patriarchal groups, often invaders, deposed and suppressed goddess worship, sometimes with wholesale massacre. Like Marija Gimbutas—the archaeologist whose work would soon light up the field—Stone referred to evidence of widespread goddess worship throughout the Neolithic and early historic period.

FOUR

THE SACRED FEMALE

The room was filled to overflowing. It was sometime in the mid 1970s and I had come to hear religious historian Anne Barstow tell us about a sacred female from the prehistoric past. I muscled my way through people crowding into the door so I could stand at the back of the room. I remember Barstow's eyes being lit with fire as she talked. Her evidence of a prehistoric goddess came from the murals and artifacts on an ancient town in central Turkey called Çatalhöyük, a site so old (7,000-5,000 BCE) that it stood among the first human settlements of human evolution, during the Agricultural Revolution. I did not realize how hungry I was for such information. The audience was electrified by the news and in the following days, we female students whispered among ourselves that perhaps women had invented agriculture. I say "whispered" because it seemed rather outrageous at the time to suggest that women had any such prominent role in the development of civilization.

Barstow's address was based on the work of British archaeologist James Mellaart, from his excavations in Çatalhöyük. She has written "I know what I felt when I first saw the ruins of a shrine at Çatalhöyük....The goddess figure .... her legs stretched wide, giving birth, was a symbol of life and creativity such as I had not seen in the Western Church."[7]

This was a female deity of life as well as death, of fecundity and rebirth. Above all, she was a personification of nature, sometimes flanked by leopards or dancing with deer. At other times, she wore the dress of a raven, the birds that would eat corpses exposed to the elements in excarnation (defleshing) ceremonies.

When British archaeologist James Mellaart excavated this site in the 1960s, he startled the world with his description of goddess figures[8] plastered onto the walls of the rooms, their legs opened wide, their arms held up and out at the sides in what is called an "orant" posture—bent at the elbow with hands facing outward. The figure conveys a joyous, jumping quality and there were many of them, Mellaart said, that were associated with nearby bull's heads.

"The frequency with which the goddess is shown associated with wild animals probably reflects her ancient role as the provider of game for a hunting population, and as patroness of the hunt," he wrote.

By far, the most evocative figure from Çatalhöyük is the famous seated goddess, her ample figure resting between two leopard figures that form the arms of the chair. Her hands rest on the animal bodies, suggesting a powerful association between the sacred female and wild animals. The head of a skull rests on the floor between her legs, perhaps indicating that life and death were brought together at Çatalhöyük in the image of a sacred female.

Mellaart wrote of these images: "As a probable goddess of death, she is accompanied by a bird of prey, possibly a vulture, and her grim expression suggests old age, the crone of later mythology. Her symbols of death, vultures, are frequently represented in early shrines," Mellaart said, proposing that the care with which the dead were buried—in the houses under platforms—reflected a belief in the regeneration of life.

At Çatalhöyük there is no evidence of human sacrifice, such as that found in later societies, as human civilization geared up for a more violent history following the development of metallurgy, weapons, armies and hierarchy.

This was not a bloody cult, said Barstow, and "it does not relate to the demonic. It does not, therefore, express two of the themes commonly associated with the female in art. It is, rather, a celebration of fecundity and rebirth, and of the beauty and strength of textiles, animals and women. And it is powerful."[9]

Female power and authority. Who among us has not struggled with these ideas? So many of our fundamental attitudes about gender—in the Western world—stem from research at premier institutions such as the University of Pennsylvania. And the elite academy tends to be especially dominated by powerful male authority. Barstow's address opened up a wedge for me, allowing me to question other rigid ideas I was encountering in academe, such as the idea that men's lives were the only drivers of human evolution.

Could women have invented agriculture, I wondered? The idea made sense because Neolithic women gathered most of the food from wild sources, while men hunted—occasionally —for big game. Still, we didn't speak too openly about it. One day, the thought slipped out at the check-out desk in the museum library. A male graduate student, overhearing us, sneered, "I suppose you're going to say that women invented the violin too!"

I was enraged. I wanted to kick in the doors and smash the windows. These were our origin stories, the very stuff of human evolution that tells us who we are as people and how we got here, and only males figured in them. That comment has stayed with me for forty years as a prime example of male bias.

ARRIVAL OF THE GREAT GODDESS

Mellaart's work was only a start. Yet to come in the 1970s, and for the next two decades, were the books on a prehistoric goddess by Marija Gimbutas, a prominent archaeologist from the University of California at Los Angeles. Born in Lithuania, Gimbutas was widely known as the first to place the origins of Indo-European peoples in an early Caucasian group called the Kurgan culture. She proposed that in prehistoric times, these Kurgan people had moved from their homeland in the Russian steppe to overtake indigenous cultures throughout Eastern Europe, bringing their language and patriarchal culture with them.

Following the Kurgan hypothesis, over two decades of writing, she would create a spectacular figure—the Great Goddess—who stood for the mystery of birth, death and the renewal of life, not only human life, but all life on earth and in the cosmos.

Gimbutas's sweeping prehistory is far and away the best story ever written about the Neolithic and the largest body of work. No other archaeologist can compare with her scope—the number of objects she analyzed, the detail, the startling interdisciplinary reach into mythology, linguistics and other sources of knowledge. She was a giant in her field.

When I first encountered her huge book, *Civilization of the Goddess*, it came to me like a lightning strike. Here was a deity on the order of the patriarchal God. Divinity belonged to me, a woman. There was a time, before male dominance, when humans broadly imagined spiritual life as female. Moreover, it was a "civilization," not just a tribe here and there.

For her material, Gimbutas used not only her own excavations but thousands of artifacts from across a broad sweep of prehistoric Europe, the Mediterranean and the Near East. Much of this material had been lying around in museum drawers since they were dug out of the earth in past decades. There were tens of thousands of these figurines, vases, pots and other artifacts, the vast majority of which had female or animal features. Few represented males.

Made of clay, ivory or, less frequently, stone, the small objects were highly stylized. Since they are mostly abstract images, they are difficult to interpret; the artists left no descriptions. The images are variable, but they do share similar traits. Most are nearly faceless, with no articulated hands or feet. The feet are often joined and pointed downward, as though to stick in the earth. Some artifacts are thin, like blades, with only slight humanoid features such as pointed breasts. Others are quite fat with exaggerated breasts, buttocks and mid sections. Once in a while, one sees a female flanked by leopards.

Each new excavation in Europe from the Prehistoric period brought up new artifacts like this. For decades, archaeologists had been calling them "Venus" figures, "fertility symbols" or "fetishes," terms that minimized their importance. The terms archaeologists used carried the annoying suggestion that the objects had been created from male sexual desire. "Fertility cult," another descriptor, dramatically limited interpretations to female birth functions.

Gimbutas turned all of that on its head when she began to publish her books identifying the artifacts as representative of a Goddess/Creatrix in prehistory: worship of the Earth and nature in female form.

> "The Goddess in all her manifestations was a symbol of the unity of all life in Nature. Her power was in water and stone, in tomb and cave, in animals and flowers.... The question of mortality was of profound concern but the deep perception of the periodicity of nature based on the cycles of the moon and the female body led to the creation of a strong belief in the immediate regeneration of life at the crisis of death. There was no simple death, only death and regeneration."[10]

Animal, plant and human forms constantly intermix in these prehistoric objects, in ways that imply few boundaries. There are snakes winding upward, trees, bees and butterflies rising from caves or tombs and sometimes a uterus. One form dissolves into another. Human bodies become part bird, snake, fish and frog. The cycles never stop turning, wrote Gimbutas, as life energy reemerges in different forms. Many artifacts carry suggestions of female sexual attributes mixed with animal features, such as the head of a bird or snake on top of a cone-shaped neck, on top of a strange-shaped body with breasts and big buttocks.

Gimbutas described this neck as phallus-like, a word that she also used when writing about a goddess figure holding a snake against her body. I like to think—setting my imagination free— that we are looking at a human reverence for sexuality and love that is embedded in plants and animals, not restricted to female imagery, but illustrated by it. There is nothing degraded about this sexuality; it is not tainted by exploitation of the female body. This is the channel through which creation occurs; therefore female forms and genitals take on spiritual qualities. The images restore dignity and centrality to the female body.

Significantly, there is no hint of violence or aggression in these prehistoric images, nor in the ideology Gimbutas created. In fact, her description paints a peaceful, cooperative portrait of human life, with intimate links between the goddess and the natural world.

As products of a male-dominant culture, we have difficulty freeing our minds from the stigma conferred on sexuality, particularly in regard to women's bodies. If you choose to see it, our human bodies—both male and female—hold a sacred quality, but women, as the childbearing sex, have a particular sacredness that has not been much in evidence since the God of the Bible gave males dominion over women and nature in the Garden of Eden. Sexuality, nakedness, breast and vagina became objects to control, if not to approach with shame. This has deeply disempowered women for 3,500 years, broadly crippling our ability to take equal positions of authority with men throughout most of written history.

By contrast, the female deity exemplified by the Neolithic goddess is embodied, deeply connected with Earth and the natural world. This is the gender that grows and nurtures new life; as such, women have unique mental and physical experiences.

Gimbutas named this deity the "Goddess/Creatrix," meaning all life in nature. When I think about living in the Neolithic, surrounded by an untamed wilderness, seeing spirits in trees and rocks, dominated by weather patterns that might arrive without warning, I can understand the blending of human and non-human life that Gimbutas envisioned. In the introduction to *Language of the Goddess,* she describes the worldview that informed her work, an "invigorating, Earth-centered, life-reverencing worldview":

The abstract, artistic images of this Goddess "cluster around…her basic functions as Giver of Life, Wielder of Death and, not less importantly, as Regeneratrix and around the Earth Mother, the Fertility Goddess young and old, rising and dying with plant life. She was the single source of all life who took her energy from the springs and wells, from the sun, moon and moist earth. This symbolic system represents cyclical, not linear, mythical time."[11]

People searching for a new form of Earth-based spirituality eagerly welcomed the incredible images and the interpretations Gimbutas provided, converging with what one observer called the fast-growing "religion of the living Goddess."

But other archaeologists were swamped, overwhelmed and outgunned. They had nothing to compare with this story, no way to combat or critique it. Gimbutas had drawn comparisons between artifacts across a wide swath of prehistoric Europe, including not only her own excavations, but others as well. Archaeologists rarely do that; their usually circumspect interpretations get buried in the layered analysis of stratigraphy on a single site. The backlash began soon after Gimbutas's death in 1994.

I had long since left Penn when that reaction began, so when I started this memoir, I had only a slim idea of the extent to which work on the Neolithic goddess had been discredited in academia. As I have moved through voluminous research over several years, I have been amazed at how consistently and thoroughly experts in the field have taken down the evidence of both Mellaart and Gimbutas, along with the whole idea of a Neolithic goddess.

"They have buried the goddess, they have scrubbed the Neolithic material clean of all trace of her," a scholar of religion wrote in a note to me. "I could hardly believe my eyes. Here's to your attempt to bring her back."

I'm fairly certain that the special heat turned on Gimbutas and the Neolithic goddess comes from resistance to the idea of an all-powerful female; resistance coming not only from patriarchal men, but also from many academic women who strongly object to the idea that females have anything special to offer the world. These are people who like to maintain that women have never had power, never had authority of a secular or religious nature in the long history of human development. In their view, the womb restricts women's importance to childbearing.

But there is a significant difference between "rule by women" and equality. Rule by women is nothing like rule by men, because women do not rule alone. Every shred of evidence I have found in the anthropological record demonstrates to me that when women had power, the culture was actually egalitarian. The terms "matriarchy" and "gender-equal societies" have been lumped together too often, creating a source of enormous confusion. Thus I will be referring here to egalitarian cultures; I do not use the word "matriarchy."

If I do nothing more than rescue egalitarian values from this maligned notion of "women's rule," I will have done enough. Equality is what I have always cared about.

FIVE

CAUSES OF MALE DOMINANCE

It was evening in the late 1970s, as I left the university museum for the day, when I first learned about the major causes of male dominance in society. I was walking with my advisor at the time, anthropologist Peggy Reeves Sanday, who had just completed a major cross-cultural study of the subject. She said that male dominance was not universal. Inherited physical differences in size and aggression did not drive gender inequality. Instead, it was caused by threats and social disruption that shifted power to men as protectors. Relief flooded my body to learn that equality between men and women had been common in the human record.

We have few ways of actually seeing how humans in the deep past organized their lives, so we rely on hundreds of tribal cultures studied over the past 200 years as examples of the way it was. Profiles of these cultures, indexed and catalogued, are the crown jewels of anthropology. They tell us about human society before westernization, migration and globalization spread a common surface over everything. Here we can see the "DNA" of culture—how child-rearing practices lead to sex roles, how food production structures equality, how the gods that people worship and the stories they tell about the origins of the human race write the scripts for male and female behavior.

Although the vast majority of these groups have disappeared into homogenous modernization, we fortunately have reports written by anthropologists, missionaries and officials of various sorts—records now kept in universities and used by scientists to write the stories of cultural creation.

A representative group of such cultures, called the Standard Cross-Cultural Sample, provided Sanday with 156 tribes spread across the globe, cultures that would tell her why some peoples created equality between the sexes while others elevated men into dominance. The results were stunning.

In only a third of the group she analyzed did the men clearly dominate women, often treating them with abuse and preventing them from holding political or economic power. Such male-dominant patterns occurred frequently in herding societies where men managed animals that were the group's main source of food. Regular warfare, invasion and migration were also significant causes. Often, women in such groups would be traded like animals from one patrilineal culture to another with no say in the matter.

At the opposite end, a different thirty percent enjoyed equality. Men and women lived, worked and ruled together, though frequently in different ways. "There is no society I know of in which the sexes give equal energy to exactly the same activities and decisions…nor have the same access to the same resources," she wrote.[12] Nevertheless, Sanday found many societies where women were decision-makers, at least as assertive as men, and where they enjoyed magical powers associated with fertility, earth and social continuity. There was no abuse of women by men in these cultures. They were egalitarian.

The middle forty percent represented a puzzle in that men acted aggressively toward women; yet the women retained a substantial measure of political or economic power. While men monopolized public positions of power and authority, women were not actually dominated and could balance male strength with their own sources of power in the community. Sanday called this pattern "mythical" male dominance, referring, among other things, to public deference toward men by women who did not actually accept the idea that men were dominant. The sexes managed to exist in a state of balanced opposition, she wrote.[13]

Mythical male dominance seemed to occur especially in cultures exposed to European influence. With traditions and livelihoods threatened by westernization, these indigenous societies may have moved into a transitional stage, caught between egalitarian and male-dominant patterns. Women almost always lost power as Europeans took control.

During the nineteenth century, for instance, Iroquois women lost economic control of land and food—a main source of their influence—when Quakers convinced Iroquois men to take up farming, which then relegated women to a purely childbearing role, according to Sanday. The intention of the Quakers was to rescue despondent men from alcoholism (the men had lost their own occupations as hunters) but in the process, Quaker influence crystalized male dominance in a formerly egalitarian society.

In sum, male dominance was highly associated with an economy based on animal husbandry and also, most prominently, with conditions of social disruption arising from migration or invasion, warfare, loss of food and other sources of stress. In these cases, power seemed to shift prominently into the hands of men, accompanied by increased control and abuse of women.

"It is easy to imagine dependence on the male world evolving when expansion, migration or social stress puts men in the position of fighting literally and figuratively to maintain an old or to forge a new sociocultural identity....For the sake of social and cultural survival, women accept real male domination. Their lives and those of their children may rest on their willingness to do so."[14] But there was a an important exception to this pattern. When a people worshipped female deities, they were less likely to resort to male dominance when bad times arrived. In fact, Sanday concluded that gender power relations most often *arose* from sacred beliefs rather than the other way around. Male gods gave birth to male dominance, but the belief in a female deity or dual male and female sacred founders seemed to provide a more egalitarian path for groups under stress.

She concluded that if belief systems emphasized "cooperation, immersion of the group in nature and the feminine principle, male dominance is unlikely to result unless the source of stress makes the fertility of women inimical to life itself" (if, for example, the group has little food).

A good example came from the Mbuti pygmies of the Congo who told stories about the forest "being asleep" when misfortune occurred. At such times, they would blow their horns to "wake it up." A cooperative people with feminine origin myths, the Mbuti relied on the forest for sustenance, seeing it as "father and mother to us." Said one old man to anthropologist Colin Turnbull, "We wake it up by singing to it, and we do this because we want it to awaken happy. Then everything will be well and good again. So when our world is going well, then also we sing to the forest because we want to share our happiness."[15]

The attitude of these simple foragers toward their natural environment strikes me with longing in this time of climate change and mass extinctions brought about by human action. We modern Americans are not pygmies, but scientific understanding of ecology demands that we find ways of "singing to the forest," to protect our resources and awaken the world. We must not put it to sleep.

From her study of tribal cultures in general, Sanday discovered a close harmony between secular and divine authority. "When the female creative principle dominates or works in conjunction with the male principle, the sexes are either integrated and equal in everyday life, or they are separate and equal. In no sense are women portrayed as being responsible for sin and the fall of man, nor are they relegated only to conception and obedience in everyday life. In some of the stories presented...it is men who are associated with the beginning of evil and women with the bringing of the first people into the world."[16]

In contrast to the Mbuti example of cooperative gentleness, many cultures—far too many—would sink into gender warfare when misfortune occurred. Sexual differences, especially the reproductive powers of women, could easily become targets when food was scarce. Controlling women and their sexuality was one way to hamper population growth.

Sanday's description of the emotional components of male dominance strike major chords in our modern experience: "Male dominance in myth and everyday life is associated with fear, conflict and strife," she wrote. "Men attempt to neutralize the power they think is inherent in women by stealing it, nullifying it or banishing it to invisibility."[17]

Food production on the part of men was a major source of male dominance.

But the same was not true for women. There were many tribes where women did most of the work in providing food, yet were thoroughly dominated and had little or no power compared to men. The glass tipped toward male dominance in these contemporary tribal groups, most of which had already been exposed to external stress, particularly from the growing threat of western culture.

I learned during these years at Penn that sexual equality is part of our long-standing inheritance—part of our cultural development as humans that extends into the far-distant past when we lived in hunting and gathering groups. And it comes with female divinity.

I also learned from these small, preindustrial societies that men fought the wars. Women could be inspired to risk life and limb against invasion or a one-time event of war and resistance, and there were occasions in the ethnographic past when they did so. But as a group women did not ordinarily risk their lives in ongoing warfare. Of all the differences that emerged from the anthropological study of gender, one of the most consistent was that "women have not willingly faced death in violent conflict."[18] It would have been counterproductive to protect the tribe by killing the ones who carried new life.

TURNING MEN INTO WARRIORS

War did not come easily to men either. They had to be traumatized in some way—desensitized—to encourage them to risk their lives for the protection of the group. This did not occur with

occasional conflict. But in cultures that were continually threatened by violence and murder, a set of child-rearing practices
evolved over time to produce aggressive, punitive male populations, generation after generation. Fathers were separated from
the rearing of their children while mothers became ever more
limited to home and family, with devalued status. Women voluntarily gave up their power for protection.

With the appearance of archaic states in Mesopotamia and
imperial armies around 3,000 BCE, stratified male-dominant cultures began to spread throughout the known world. How and why
this happened in the late stages of the Agricultural Revolution has
recently been a subject of intense scrutiny. In one of the most recent
studies,[19] Stanford University researchers discovered that stratified
societies were fundamentally unstable, with high death rates among
the lower strata, conditions that drove migration into new territory.
Strangely enough, rather than being adaptive, stratified groups were
maladaptive, the population biologists said. By contrast, egalitarian groups developed practices like sharing, which kept them better
adapted to their environment and less likely to migrate.

The Stanford research was done by computer simulations that
modeled pure forms of equal versus stratified societies under the
same environmental conditions, so it did not reflect real conditions in the human past. Nevertheless, this kind of scenario rings
true when you consider how invasion and migration set the stage
for the rapid spread of patriarchal culture. It spread, not because it
was more adaptive, but because it was more threatened internally
by potential population collapse.

THE HYPER-MASCULINE SYNDROME

Anthropologists learned a long time ago that some of these
male-dominated groups would abuse young boys in a ceremony
aimed at "turning boys into men." They would terrify them

with painful circumcision, cut them, jab their jaws with sticks, bully them and humiliate them in a seeming effort to drive out "feminine" traits or identification. Not all cultures did this. Contemporary analysis[20] identifies forty-two (about twenty-three percent) of the 186 societies in the ethnographic index that practiced painful initiations for boys. But a significant number of those where men exercised power over women seemed to need a way to instill hyper-masculinity in the boys at puberty.

The ceremonies would create cartoon versions of aggressive manhood—desensitized, female-phobic, swaggering bullies, the best description of which was written some eighty years ago by famed anthropologist Gregory Bateson. His account of the way a patrilineal, head-hunting group in New Guinea, the Iatmul,[21] turned boys into men reverberates through the decades.

The spirit of the initiation ceremony is hardly careful or serious, Bateson wrote in his ethnography, *Naven*. "It is the spirit of irresponsible bullying and swagger. In the process of scarification, nobody cares how the little boys bear their pain. If they scream, some of the initiators go and hammer on the gongs to drown the sound. The father of the little boy will perhaps stand by and watch the process, occasionally saying in a conventional way, 'That's enough! That's enough!' but no attention is paid to him."[22]

Pain is inflicted "by men who enjoy doing it and who carry out their business in a cynical, practical-joking spirit. The drinking of filthy water is a great joke and the wretched novices are tricked into drinking plenty of it. On another occasion their mouths are opened with a piece of crocodile bone and examined 'to see that they have not eaten what they ought not'...the result of the examination is invariably the discovery that the mouth is unclean; and the bone is suddenly jabbed against the boy's gums making them bleed. Then the process is repeated for the other jaw. In the ritual washing, the partly healed backs of the novices are scrubbed, and they are splashed and splashed with icy water till they are whimpering with cold and misery. The emphasis is upon making them miserable rather than clean."[23]

This goes on for a week, with different groups of initiators earning pride points off each other for their savagery, Bateson wrote. If one group thought they perhaps had gone too far, another group would ridicule them for being lenient, at which point the lenient ones "hardened their hearts and performed the episode with some extra savagery."

During the merciless hazing, the boys "are spoken of as the 'wives' of the initiators, whose penes they are made to handle." Such shaming of them as "wives" and "women" creates a "strongly negative attitude toward the female ethos of the tribe," said Bateson—an ethos that was by tradition submissive to the men. By plunging young males into sudden and violent submission, the novices rebelled against it and became sharply anti-feminine in behavior.

This kind of introduction to adulthood fits boys "admirably for the irresponsible histrionic pride and buffoonery which is characteristic" of men's lives among the Iatmul. The young men confront an adult life where they will face the daily threat of being killed and scalped by feuding members of a neighboring tribe.

"As in other cultures a boy is disciplined so that he may be able to wield authority, so on the Sepik (the river which was home to these people) he is subjected to irresponsible bullying and ignominy so that he becomes what we should describe as an overcompensating, harsh man—whom the natives describe as a 'hot' man,"[24] Bateson concluded.

Nearly all these kinds of ceremonies occurred in cultures where boys were reared almost completely by their mothers, sleeping with them in the same quarters, while the fathers, distant and authoritarian, slept in the men's house. Theoretically, it was a small step from these tribal ceremonies to Freudian thought during the early twentieth century when psychologists were considering the impact on men of being reared mostly by women in a patriarchal culture. By the 1950s, we had experienced decades of growing up with absent fathers and all-too-present mothers who had little release from the household. The parallel with these tribal cultures was not perfect, but it was evocative.

LOSS OF FATHERS

Anthropologists John and Beatrice Whiting made a lasting impact on the field with their classic studies of family sleeping arrangements in patriarchal cultures. Young boys growing up in cultures where men both dominated women and slept apart from them would first develop a feminine identity, they said. Then, realizing that men had the power but feeling hostile or distant from fathers, and having no easy identification with the male role, the boys would need some radical shift into a masculine mode at puberty. Frightening, scarring, painful ritual carried out by adult men gave entrance to manhood, making sure the boys suppressed all signs of former feminine traits. Since they had virtually no fathering, especially no nurturing experience with fathers, the switch left a hyper-aggressive, insensitive version of masculinity.

Why their sexual identity had to be formed in such pain, however, continues to be controversial. Many societies, for instance, would ritually mark adulthood for young boys, without putting them through such emotional and physical trauma as Bateson described. Some believe that the existence of warfare required such toughening. Others now challenge that but say that the need to make the boys highly obedient to male authority was the critical factor.

Whatever the case in tribal culture, it was a short step from research like this to images of boot camp in modern-day warfare.

"A male initiation ceremony has elements similar to basic army training in our own society,"wrote Carol and Melvin Ember in 2010.[25] "In our society, one hears people say that military service makes 'boys into men.' We take the young men who volunteer for military service away from their families. We seclude them for a time from the possibility of dating women. We cut their hair severely....We give them a distinctive set of clothes.... And we subject them to tough drill sergeants and grueling physical and emotional stress. These various experiences seem to lead the young men to develop strong solidarity with their buddies, to become outwardly tough and brave, and to identify with the aggressors (in this case, with their noncom superiors) and incorporate those aggressors' rules, attitudes, and values."

I learned about the Iatmul in the years when protests roiled through the streets of America against an illegitimate war in Vietnam. Drafted, the young men were being sent against their will to risk their lives in a cause they spurned. I could imagine them packed off to a camp where they were abused so that they would cooperate in having their legs and arms blown off. Why? To protect us? Who? Women and children?

The role of men in the patriarchy was never more clear. As bad as it was for women to be subdued or sexually assaulted, we were in some sense the privileged gender, the people who could not be used as killers. Moreover, we were allowed to be fully human, not traumatized so that we would become emotionally desensitized, thus willing to risk our lives for protection of the group.

I have never forgotten this lesson. Men were not the problem for women. The culture that imposed male dominance was a problem for us both. And in our stratified society, not all men carried the burden. It was poor men, lower class men, who were sent to war; the educated escaped that fate.

When the compulsory military draft ended for American men in 1973, millions were freed to become themselves. For the first time in my generation, men were no longer required to go through training to kill and be killed, a process of "masculinization" based on humiliation, dominance and suppression of sensitivity. So the way of the world, the way of "becoming a man" was radically rerouted. Maybe they could become good fathers?

Not so fast. Corporate America still had an iron grip on the masculine ethos.

Working longer and longer hours, becoming ever more "productive," men—and now women who joined them in the workplace—had no time for children. When pressed about the needs of family, corporate leaders tended to give the same answer I heard from the executive editor of the *Philadelphia Inquirer* at the time: "I'm willing to give parental leave to women, but not to men."

And it stayed that way in the following decades.

CONTEMPORARY CONCERNS ABOUT MASCULINITY

The questions about masculinity plague the nation still, considering the nature of the authoritarian administration in power as I write, and the questions about how men evolve in a culture striving toward gender equality. In a 2020 study of boys from well-to-do families, Peggy Orenstein has recorded how they brutalize each other to carry on the traditions of control and command masculinity.[26] Somehow, the need to maintain so-called "toxic masculinity" gets transmitted through the culture, even without brutal initiations from older men.

In a 2016 article[27] in *The New York Times*, Andrew Reiner wrote, "Despite the emergence of the metrosexual and an increase in stay at home dads, tough guy stereotypes die hard. As men continue to fall behind women in college, while outpacing them four to one in the suicide rate, some colleges are waking up to the fact that men may need to be taught to think beyond their own stereotypes."

Such questions about masculinity go to the heart of our patriarchal system, raising every political division on the map. Here's a recent quote from the online right-wing magazine *American Thinker*:[28]

"The feminist hatred for masculinity is only another tool in the toolbox of communism. Masculinity tends to make a man individualistic. Individualistic men are capitalists, not communists. They are men who cherish individual liberty, and they rely on themselves rather than on government. Self-reliance is a four-letter word for leftists, and masculine men are generally self-reliant. Beta males like Pajama Boy rely on government, and such modern men, devoid of any semblance of masculinity, are ideal for leftist indoctrination."

Fear of a "genderless" world, led by feminists, in which men are denigrated was more poignantly expressed by David French, columnist for the *National Review*.[29] In recalling the good old days when men were men, French wrote, just before Trump was elected president:

"Trump's masculinity is a cheap counterfeit of the masculinity that's truly threatening to the cultural Left: man not as predator but as protector, the "sheepdog" of *American Sniper* fame. This is the brave man, the selfless man who channels his aggression and sense of adventure into building a nation, an economy, and—yes—a family. This is the man who kicks down doors in Fallujah or gathers a makeshift militia to rush hijackers in the skies above Pennsylvania. Or, to choose a more mundane—though no less important—example: This is the man who packs up the household to take a chance on a new job, models strength for his family when life turns hard, teaches his son to stand against bullies on the playground, and lives at all times with dignity and honor."

It's a beautiful memory—the dream of John Wayne. What a wonderful portrait: the brave, strong and selfless man who lives with dignity and honor. It's just that getting there does not rely on formulas for masculinity born out of warfare. It depends on a more complicated process—becoming truly and fully human as individuals with compassion for others. I have no quarrel with men or women who choose soldiering because that's what they need in their lives; being forced to kill and be killed is another matter altogether.

In the decades since the end of the draft, I thrilled to watch young men hike on back-country trails carrying children on their backs. It would move me to tears, seeing them have the opportunity to care for the little ones. There was no sense whatsoever of a loss of masculinity, just a beautiful memory of fathering. I dream of what it would be like if all of us, men and women together, had the chance to be fully human, in love with ourselves and each other.

SIX

THROUGH THE UNDERWORLD

The big, three-story townhouse in Center City, Philadelphia, echoed with the voices of those who had left. My housemates on the third floor had moved out. My partner Don had moved out, and after a few weeks, his daughter Valerie had followed him. I was alone. Light filtered down the twenty-foot wall where a grand staircase descended from the second floor to the big living room, a metaphor for my coming descent into the mythological underworld. It was 1978. The dark of winter had come.

SEPARATION AND ILLNESS

As quickly as I could, I moved into a small sub-basement apartment on Society Hill, along a cobblestoned street on which Benjamin Franklin had probably walked. It was charming, imbued with the history of the founding of our nation. I joined an ecstatic dance group, vibrating with energy that I borrowed from some unknown source. I also scored a temporary job editing manuscripts in archaeology at Penn. Then, while dancing one night, I collapsed onto the floor and could not get up.

Every joint in my body rebelled in what doctors called "polyarthritis." My knees swelled until they were about thirteen inches around and I couldn't walk—one doctor told me I might never walk again. There was inflammation everywhere, likely influenced, if not caused, by a huge shot of hormones I had been given recently to stop me from hemorrhaging after a miscarriage. I had to go to bed and stay there, editing while propped up on pillows. But I could swim, and the health club was only a couple of blocks away. My daily routine included hobbling to the club, swimming and sitting in the hot tub, plus taking twelve aspirin a day. It took six months, but I recovered.

Back at the museum, in another sub-basement devoted to Mayan archaeology, I helped epigrapher Chris Jones pull together his work on Mayan stelae and the glyphs engraved on the sides of the monoliths. He was a wonderful man, one of the most enlightened, beautiful people I've ever met—generous, warm and enthralled by the mysterious script, not yet deciphered, left by these ancient people. We would sit together as darkness fell outside, puzzling over the immense cycles of the Long Count, millions of years, by which the Maya viewed time.

Surrounding our solitary work in that room, bookshelves lined every wall holding more than a dozen volumes of unpublished work from the Tikal excavation. They held exquisite drawings and descriptions in big blue binders from decades ago, waiting for someone or something to move William Coe, the lead excavator on the 1950s Tikal expedition, to publish his trove. It had been twenty years since the expedition ended and the authors were dying.

Jones had come to Penn to help Coe move this enormous archive into the public realm.

Coe's approach was to focus on the stratigraphy of a site, with minimal interpretation, reflecting the scientism of archaeology and the fear of many to create interpretations about the people under study.

Jones was the first to publish on this material, the volume entitled *Monuments and Inscriptions of Tikal*.[30] I am proud that I helped him with it. But my own work as an editor was coming to an end. We finished the first draft of Jones's book, and Coe was not interested in publishing any more volumes.[31]

I needed to move on. My dreams could not have been more clear. In one memorable image, I was buried in a deep subterranean cave, sitting in my old red Volkswagen Beetle while a lover advised me to get out of there. I knew I had to do something big—something I never imagined I could do—if I were to escape from the cave. I was forty years old and had nothing to show for it. I had no family, no husband (nor lover at the time), no money, no job, no children. I bicycled through Philadelphia's snowy winter because I didn't own a car. The ice and slush crunched under my tires as I repeated the mantra: "I will not be defeated. I will not be defeated."

I went to see Gene Roberts at the *Inquirer* to plead for the return of my job. He said he couldn't do that because of the Guild involvement in my case, but he did offer me a monthly stipend for regular contributions to the paper's Sunday magazine, called *Today Magazine*. So, for a small sum that paid rent and food, I set out to write magazine articles, selling them for additional income through the Knight Ridder syndicate that had papers in San Jose, Miami and other major cities.

MAGAZINE JOURNALISM AND ANTHROPOLOGY

It was a sufficient living, though still insecure. I traveled to Guatemala to do a story on the disappearance of Mayan culture, following the trail set out for me by Jones. And I went to Alaska in the middle of January to write an article on traumatic shocks to Eskimo identity from a sudden infusion of oil money and modernity into the ancient Arctic hunter-gatherer culture of the Inuit.

The story on the North Slope was one of the most fascinating and consequential I had ever covered. Native people there were plagued by alcoholism and many of them, particularly young men, were killing themselves with drink. I heard that young men in their prime years, 35 years old, would walk out into the snow with a bottle of whiskey and drink the whole thing while freezing to death. Or groups of young people would wander along the beaches, aimlessly, their former patterns of life totally disrupted by modern change produced by oil money. The whale meat they used to catch in canoes was being supplied in the frozen meat department of the grocery store.

Alcoholism was at epidemic proportions and city officials at Barrow were alarmed enough to hire two researchers from the University of Pennsylvania to evaluate the problem. One of them was my professor, anthropologist/psychiatrist Edward Foulkes. I went with him to Alaska to get the story for the *Inquirer* as he conveyed his results to the Inuit. Meanwhile, his co-author, sociologist Samuel Klausner, held a press conference in New York, warning that the Eskimos were "practically committing suicide" with alcohol and could become extinct as a culture before the oil ran out. The story ran on the front page of the *New York Times*[32] (as well as in other media) and was broadcast over the loudspeakers in a Barrow grocery store.

Foulkes and I flew straight north, disembarking in Barrow, where the temperature was below zero and snow swirled through the air on the winds of a pitch-black night. As we disembarked, we learned that the town's residents were up in arms and ready to riot on his arrival. They felt they had been shamed in front of the entire country and were furious at the news release, which had been requested by Barrow officials.

We entered the airport lounge tentatively, where locals conferred furiously with Foulkes. I looked around and breathed a sigh of relief. No riot yet. The gentle Inupiat had other ways to express their fury and it wasn't violence, but it was effective. They ostracized Foulkes and me—a reporter who could give them even more unwelcome attention.

I had two days to gather the information and no one would talk to me. I remember sitting alone in Barrow's Top of the World Cafe with stony silence all around. People in the cafe focused intensely on their plates and would not acknowledge my approach. Not a good sign.

On the second day, with time on my hands, I decided to visit the highest point in Barrow to watch the sun peeking above the horizon for a moment. There I met a local journalist who took pity on me, promising to introduce me to some assertive young men who would give me a story. I went with him and got one of the best stories of my life, about the disastrous effects of westernization on people who had been put through a time machine, shot forward 10,000 years in two decades, from hunting and gathering their food into the uselessness of urban life without meaningful work. My article was published in the *Inquirer* under the title, "Dark Nights of the Soul Under the Midnight Sun."[33]

This resumption of journalism was not lost on my academic advisors.

Confronting me in the hall one day, one of my graduate advisors, William Davenport, wanted to know: "Are you ever going to be a scholar?"

I looked at him mutely, thinking, "Uh, probably not."

He said, "I'm going to stop talking with you, if you don't get serious!"

"Okay," I replied. I didn't want Davenport to stop talking to me. I would get serious.

I knew I had to do something big to kick my career onto a higher plane. I had to write a book; I also had to write a PhD thesis. Maybe I could do the two together! In retrospect, this idea was slightly delusional, but at the time it seemed that I could collect the necessary data, write a popular book and then turn it into a PhD thesis. At least I would try, and with the help of my advisors, I began to map out the research methods.

This was hardly an easy decision; I didn't really believe I had the capacity to write a book. But I was up against the wall of fate. Do it, or go down in defeat. I had left California with the optimistic aim of "making my name" and then getting married, having achieved some degree of immunity against the typical women's lot of being limited to the domestic sphere of life, devastation I saw in my own mother and other women of my age. I planned to define myself and then become a wife and mother.

Well, that had not worked out so well. Thirteen years later, I was living alone on chicken feed. The stories I wrote, though well-written and well-researched, were printed on news stock destined for landfill. In the pre-Internet age, only a book would survive for another day. I wanted to return to my native state, but not this way, in defeat. I thought I could still adopt a child, but without money or family around, adoption would be risky.

LEAPING OFF THE CLIFF

The decision was made at some level below my rational brain. I just had to write a book, whether I thought it was possible or not. I had a subject close to my own experience that I believed would be relevant to women in 1980—sex in the workplace. What were women doing about romantic attachment as they entered a male-dominated workplace? Was anyone paying the same price I had paid? I could do an ethnography in modern culture, I thought. But where? Study whom?

One day, sitting in the Center City health club where I hung out every day, I saw something astonishing. Normally, women came to the club from work dressed in traditional feminine clothing. Suddenly I saw a sea change. One after another, women walked into the club's social lounge in blue suits with little white ties. The era of "dress for success" had arrived, bringing dramatic change in the way women presented themselves. As an anthropologist in training, I knew this meant a change of identity and behavior. Many were women working in the financial world. Now I had the subculture to study: Wall Street.

Through friends in Philadelphia's writing community, I obtained a contract to write the book for William Morrow publishers and set out to interview women in the financial districts of New York and San Francisco, many of whom had been elevated from "female" work as secretaries to "male" work as financial professionals. My advisors at Penn helped me prepare the interview method so that it would give me both quantifiable data and rich personal detail.

I planned the research so it would take me to San Francisco where I could spend some time testing out my relationship with the new California, so unlike the one I had left. Once in the city, my spirits lifted as I observed good-natured public behavior, like the time a bus driver pulled over to jump out and get himself a hamburger, while we riders waited, chatting and laughing. I'd never seen anything like that before. In Philadelphia, I thought, they would have had his head on a stake. Yes, I decided, I would move to California as soon as I could.

Back in the East, I analyzed my results, discovering significant attitudes toward reproduction that paired with a woman's interpretation of "feminine" as strong or weak. When "feminine" was seen as weak, women did not want to have children; by comparison, a "strong" interpretation of that gender identity came with the desire to reproduce.

Now I had a significant finding and a box full of interview tapes to transcribe. My process would work, but I had to descend into the underworld before I was through.

RETREAT TO THE TOP OF A HILL

My teeth rotted the winter I wrote that book—along with the undercarriage of my car. Metal does not do well on salty roads in snowy climates. I lost my new love, who couldn't stand the poverty I had voluntarily undertaken in moving away from cohabitation with him to a lonely perch on top of a hill outside the urban area. One day, as a monster snowstorm approached the little township of Birchrunville where I lived, he called to tell me he was not coming to visit. We were done. He had found someone else. I felt numb with grief and isolation, but I had to write, had to finish. When the need for contact became overwhelming, I would call and plead with my former lover. Self-respect was not even an issue; I did what I had to do.

My mother came through with a small monthly check to replace the stipend I had given up at the *Philadelphia Inquirer*. It was just enough to live on, provided I kept heating oil consumption to a minimum. I shared a little tenant's cabin with a young couple, just married. The estate had long been abandoned, and the main house—actually a classic old mansion—down the hill was all boarded up. We were surrounded on all sides by gorgeous but empty fields and forests that once sustained race horses. The area was still full of racing aficionados who loved the sport. You could spot them from our windows wearing red jackets, following the hounds, jumping over broken-down white fences, riding English saddles. I sometimes wondered what century I had entered.

We were all poor, the young couple and I, so we kept the oil burners at fifty degrees that winter, supplemented with kerosene heaters that we moved from room to room. My writing desk was in a lean-to attached to the back of the cabin where, wrapped up in blankets, I huddled over a Selectric typewriter. When my car broke down in the snow, I repaired it myself. As I worked under the hood in subfreezing temperatures one day, a kind stranger came along to help. Together, we got the car running again.

I don't know how I completed that journey. But I do understand that when you set out to cross the ocean, there is no turning back. It seems in retrospect that my time followed a three-day cycle, two days of near psychosis followed by a day of clarity when I would suddenly know what to write, and then the confusion would return to be followed by clarity again. In this way, the book was written. When I sent off the manuscript on an airplane to New York, it was two years late. I did not know whether my editor would still publish it; we hadn't communicated in a long time. But I knew in my heart that I had done my very best; there was nothing left to do but wait. I felt complete.

SEVEN

RESURFACING

That winter in 1985 I lived quietly and simply. One night, the moon outside my window lit up the snowfield that stretched far down the hill behind my cabin. I was drawn out the door as though by magic to see, directly above me, the full moon in a cloudless sky, framed by the bare branches of two trees. I was transfixed. I could not stop looking at the moon and as I looked, the sense of a transcendent presence came over me. From the moon, across the sky to the horizon below me, I sensed a benevolent spirit. It was palpable. It existed. I stayed for what seemed like a long time, in that bright, moonlit night, washed with the sense of an enduring universal love.

After I sent off the manuscript, three months passed before I heard a reply. My roommates had moved out and I was alone. I remember thinking, as I lay in bed, that Jesus had said even the sparrows of the sky would be taken care of, why not me? I don't mean to say that my Christian faith was revived. The divinity that stirred in me was feminine, a deity no longer dressed in Grecian robes, but imbedded in the natural environment. She had no name, no image, but there was a new acceptance within me, a sense of self that was me and also more than me, perhaps a willingness to see my femaleness as potent and enduring. I realized that I might never return to life from this faraway place and that would be all right.

The snows melted and thunderstorms arrived. One of those storms came to rest directly above my roof, a black thunderhead that spewed lightning at the same time it boomed. Because the lightning and thundering were simultaneous, I knew the source was as close as it could get. I also knew there were no lightning rods to redirect the energy away from the cabin. I felt immersed.

And I was nude. I don't remember why I hadn't dressed; perhaps because I was alone in a sultry environment.

Suddenly, the house was hit by a blinding flash and the lights went out. A blue flame shot into the middle of the room as it pitched a lamp cord through the air from a burned-out socket. It seemed as though the blue flash was two feet long right into the middle of the room. I screamed and screamed. Never had I seen such elemental power so close. You could call it goddess power, but I don't. God, goddess, it doesn't matter what titles you use. Naming is a parlor game for humans. This was the basic energy of the universe, and it was exhilarating.

The storm passed without lasting damage. One morning the phone rang. It was my editor at William Morrow. "The book is wonderful," she said. I sucked in my breath.

She went on, telling me that she had stayed up most of the night reading it and would have it published within the year. Rewriting would be minimal, but an index was needed. She thought it would be a big book. I could hardly believe my ears.

I began to surface from the bottom of the world, clothed in a new identity: author, soon to be adjunct professor of women's studies. With a book titled *The Third Sex: The New Professional Woman*,[34] I was ahead of the curve in discovering how professional jobs were affecting feminine identity and reproductive choices. The media attention was gratifying, especially after a book review in *The New York Times*.[35] I moved out of Birchrunville to Princeton and got an adjunct teaching position in women's studies at Rutgers University.

There were moments of fame—peculiar and fleeting. I remember the thrill of seeing my book featured in the front window of Doubleday's bookstore on Fifth Avenue. I walked around that day thinking I had "made it" in New York. I was interviewed on the radio by Terry Gross. Requests for lectures arrived.

There was an invitation from Ted Koppel's television program, "Nightline." They wanted me to appear on the show! But I was out of town when the call came. Listening to phone messages on my answering machine, I heard the publicist at Morrow call frantically several times before the final message: "Sorry, it's too late."

In some sense, I was glad I missed the interview. My message was rather sardonic. This was 1986 and many women I studied were coping with enormous difficulties in pulling together a full life of work and home. What was I going to tell those who had devoted their lives to careers while missing out on having children? Go to the gym?

As for me, I still had holes in my shoes and I had lost my love. To my feminine identity, framed in the 1950s, the romantic deprivation felt like punishment for becoming too prominent, for competing with a man for creative success. The day my book review appeared in *The New York Times,* I read it and moaned. An annoyed roommate heard me as we stood in the kitchen:

"How can you be depressed?" he scolded. "Anyone else would die for such a review. What's wrong with you?" I burst out crying.

A year later, I boarded a train back to California carrying six suitcases, with 1,000 pounds of belongings to follow by van. I was fifty years old and my aim was to secure a base for the rest of my life. I had $3,000 in total assets. The book, while giving me a critical new identity, had not brought in any money.

GOING HOME

During my 23-year odyssey through the great Northeast, California had been transformed. It seemed completely unlike the one I had left. In the early sixties, I had watched development explode along new freeways while my friends disappeared into suburbs. I saw nothing attractive about adult life for a woman. It seemed boring, stifling.

I could not have known that my state was a handful of years from a revolution that would make northern California a kind of frontier for spiritual change. Psychedelic drugs, war resistance, and the human potential movement were all part of that.

The first thing I wanted to do was reestablish connections with my family of origin: my sister Janet and her family; my mother, aunts and cousins. They made it easy, welcoming me home. My aunt picked me up in Sacramento at the end of my cross-country trip by train from Philadelphia. My cousin loaned me his 1964 Ford Falcon, which was something of a challenge on the hills of San Francisco. When you worked the clutch at a red light, the car rolled backward fast. My mother, still living in Pasadena, was happy to have me home and my sister gave me much-needed consolation while I recovered from a love affair gone bad. I knew they loved me.

Then, there was the stunning physical beauty of the place.

I remember driving in 1987 through the Caldecott Tunnel in the East Bay hills, emerging suddenly to see San Francisco Bay and, in the distance, Mt. Tamalpais, against the setting sun. I thought, *This can't be right! People don't live in beauty like this; it isn't real!* With a temperate climate, well-educated people from many parts of the globe, and an affinity for Asian culture and spiritual practice, the Bay Area seemed then—and remains—privileged ground. I could get used to this. I moved into a house share up near the East Bay hills. The deck jutted out over a deep canyon where the fog drifted in and out and where I watched my house-mate do Tai Chi, his black clad arms moving slowly in the cool air.

I sought out Esalen, a home of spiritual development along the Big Sur coast, with one of the most glorious ocean cliff scenes in the world. This was the world of personal growth that I had missed in the East. I still did not have much money, but who needed it, living in a place like this? The outdoors was free. I lost the sense of urgency I'd had in the East, where it seemed one had to live fast and furiously during the four months of the year when the weather was decent. In the Bay Area, the sun was nearly always present.

Professionally, I threw in the towel as a journalist and took a job with the University of California at Berkeley as a news officer.

I had to make my life secure, so I had no choice but to get a job in a place that supplied retirement and health benefits. Still, I did not want to do this kind of work full time, so I negotiated part-time employment and also taught women's studies as an adjunct professor at Mills College. I never regretted skipping the PhD program at Penn, but lack of a doctorate ruled out any full-time faculty position. I kept my sense of professional agency by teaching part-time. And women were on the move in the '90s.

THE FOURTH WORLD CONFERENCE ON WOMEN, CHINA

In 1995, I joined a contingent of Mills College faculty to attend the Fourth World Conference on Women in Beijing, China—an awesome experience bringing together 35,000 women from cities, towns and small villages around the world. The nongovernmental program was unique, providing space for hundreds of events each day where groups of women could tell their stories, a kaleidoscope of voices punctuated by major speakers whose political and intellectual gravitas stunned me. I became aware that American women were not leading this women's movement. An even more vigorous energy was coming from the developing world.

Most memorable perhaps was sitting on steps in the aisle of a packed auditorium listening to Hillary Clinton give her now famous speech, "Women's Rights are Human Rights." I was lucky to get in. The auditorium accommodated only 1,700 and the pack of women waiting that morning practically broke down the building's glass walls before the doors opened. It was raining as it had been all week, creating a sea of mud at the convention and a sea of umbrellas outside the auditorium.

Then there were the Chinese soldiers. The Chinese government, spooked by the thought of 35,000 women in one place, had tried to move the conference out of its country. There were

Chinese rumors that we might march unclothed in the streets. Unsuccessful at moving the event, officials built a whole new town, called Hauirou, thirty-five miles from Beijing, for those of us attending the huge nongovernmental organization (NGO) component of the UN conference, so that we could be isolated from the Chinese population. The cement-block high-rises where we stayed were put up so fast that floors never drained properly and the rainwater that flowed in ran the wrong way. Moreover, to get into our residences, we had to march past a phalanx of young soldiers (of both sexes) holding guns. But it was all good. By the end of the week, we were chatting and smiling with the soldiers, their discipline totally gone.

When I arrived back at Berkeley, my office mates rushed up to me wanting to know that I was all right. All they knew from the conference was what they heard on the news: mud, soldiers and threats. Nothing was reported about the truly amazing aspects of the conference. I was more acutely aware than ever how negatively charged the news always is. Every bizarre, horrible event that happens anywhere on the globe is brought to our doorstep every morning, totally skewing our understanding of the true state of the nation and world. I was taught in journalism school that "good news is not news." That has always been true. News is, by its nature, negative.

I don't blame the media for this tendency; it is part of the basic nature of human communication. Even rumors, in places where professional news is not allowed, have a negative slant. They are meant to alert us to danger and that's what the news does every day. We are constantly surrounded by threat and there's no solution for it but to treat news as a kind of necessary poison. Take it in small amounts. You will rarely hear about love and cooperation through this medium. It doesn't sell and it's hard to write.

The digital revolution arrived in full force during the time I worked at the university. They say it made us all more productive. Maybe so, but it also nailed us to our seats. Instead of walking across campus to meet and talk with a source, we cleared stories by email. Multitasking—reading screens while talking on the phone, handling more than one story at a time—speeded up. The mind raced faster; the body moved less; the resulting energy stoked up the nervous system. At one point in the late '90s, I knew I had to find a way to calm down my body and mind so I began to investigate meditation, finding my way eventually to the Zen Center in Berkeley. It was an enormous relief to stare at a blank white wall and do nothing but breathe. I began a meditation practice that has carried me through to the present day.

Meanwhile, at Berkeley, I encountered a totally different version of the goddess than I had encountered twenty years earlier at Penn. This one was both loving *and frightening*.

EIGHT

THE GODDESS OF LOVE

I am floating nude in a pool of hot mineral water staring up into the night sky as three friends hold me above water. I feel myself lifting out of my body and flying among the stars as though I am levitating. The bliss I feel is a product of a three-day workshop I have just completed on sex, love and intimacy, held by the Human Awareness Institute at Harbin Hot Springs, a clothing-optional resort in northern California. I have truly, for the first time, after more than half a century of life, discovered what it is like to love in a boundless, unlimited way, connected to body and mind.

I grew up with a sense of estrangement from my genitals. They were not spoken about, not seen, not touched. I thought they were dirty. Masturbation was off limits, as I discovered one day when my mother found me in a compromising position. Since I did not become a mother myself, I had no powerful way in adulthood to revise this ancient patriarchal attitude toward my female sexuality—that it must be hidden away and controlled. So it took decades until I came to realize in a human awareness workshop that the vagina is beautiful. Female sex organs are precious, even sacred. They are the avenue of life.

The ancients knew this, judging by their artistic depiction of the female body in thousands of artifacts rescued from the dirt by archaeologists who called them "Venus" figures.

But we also have a more direct way of learning about the pre-patriarchal reverence for the female body. We can read the poetry written at the dawn of history about the goddess Inanna.

Inanna emerged into history engraved on clay tablets as the goddess of love.

She was not the only deity in Mesopotamia, as humans began

keeping records of their gods, but she was the most important one—the first goddess in written history. Over more than 1,000 years of her mythological ascendancy, Inanna gathered all the powers of the other gods into her complex persona and came to be known as the Queen of Heaven and Earth.

As a lover, Inanna exuded sexuality, taking pride in her female genitals. Words translated from cuneiform tablets make her pleasure explicit: As Inanna begins a journey to the god of wisdom where she collects the "*me*" (a Sumerian word that refers to godlike powers and principles), she leans against an apple tree:

> *When she leaned against the apple tree, her vulva was wondrous to behold.*
>
> *Rejoicing at her wondrous vulva, the young woman Inanna applauded herself.* [36]

In a later hymn anticipating her union with her future husband, the shepherd Dumuzi, Inanna speaks:

> *I bathed for the wild bull,*
>
> *I bathed for the shepherd Dumuzi,*
>
> *I perfumed my sides with ointment,*
>
> *I coated my mouth with sweet-smelling amber,*
>
> *I painted my eyes with kohl.*
>
> *He shaped my loins with his fair hands,*
>
> *The shepherd Dumuzi filled my lap with cream and milk,*
>
> *He stroked my pubic hair,*

He watered my womb.

He laid his hands on my holy vulva,

He smoothed my black boat with cream,

He quickened my narrow boat with milk,

He caressed me on the bed.

Now I will caress my high priest on the bed,

I will caress the faithful shepherd Dumuzi,

I will caress his loins, the shepherdship of the land,

I will decree a sweet fate for him.[37]

No goddess has ever represented the joy of eros more exuberantly than Inanna, who was open and public about such pleasures. All the more so because sex and sexuality were sacred manifestations of the driving energy of the universe; vulva and womb were holy.

Inanna's story is particularly relevant today. She was a goddess of nature, but not of motherhood. Sexual arousal was not directed toward pregnancy, but was instead an expression of the energies flowing through the universe—the "nature of the life force." Her story aligns with our urgent needs to save the natural environment from severe global threats while reducing human procreation. For women and men, she was a supreme example of unfettered female power.

Inanna's traits bring to us a detailed portrait of female divinity before the religions of Abraham and before patriarchy destroyed such evidence—a portrait brought vividly to life by Jungian analyst Betty De Shong Meador, who wrote that Inanna's[38] "arousal and sexuality is a blessing that engenders growth and prosperity of every kind....Inanna approaches sexual arousal with abandon, with revelry, with delight. She is a goddess of play and her celebrations were noisy, costumed, song and dance, musical, carnivalesque affairs. She relishes teasing, caricature, flirtation, breaking the boundaries. She gets her way."[39]

Others who have translated and interpreted Inanna's hymns and poems have, by their own admission, fallen in love with Inanna. Folklorist Diane Wolkstein and cuneiformist Samuel Noel Kramer talk about their mutual admiration for this goddess, who brings to us "the world's first love story, two thousand years older than the Bible—tender, erotic, shocking, and compassionate." It is a "sacred story that has the intention of bringing its audience to a new spiritual place. With Inanna, we enter the place of exploration: the place where not all energies have been tamed or ordered."[40]

A MIND-BLOWING ENCOUNTER

I met this extraordinary goddess when I was a news officer at the University of California at Berkeley and had the honor of meeting Betty Meador and publicizing her work. While working at the university, Meador had had the ancient language newly translated by Berkeley's Sumerian scholar, Daniel Foxvog. She then interpreted the poems anew, telling a new and marvelous story about the first author in history, a Sumerian priestess named Enheduanna.

As high priestess of the temple at Ur in the late third millennium BCE, appointed by her father King Sargon, Enheduanna was in a unique position to create and expand Inanna's mythological power. She did so through a series of poems, captured on clay tablets, that alternately plead for mercy and exalt the powers of the goddess, powers that grew as did Enheduanna in the decades she served in her priestly functions. Her poems and spiritual authority, preserved in this early writing, outlasted her life by many centuries.

The goddess that emerges through Enheduanna's poetry (as interpreted by Meador) is phenomenal—powerful, fearless, sometimes cruel and uncaring. Enheduanna calls out to her:

> *"I plead with you*
> *I say STOP*
> *the bitter hating heart and sorrow*
>
> *my Lady*
> *what day will you have mercy*
> *how long will I cry a moaning prayer*
> *I am yours*
> *why do you slay me"* [41]

At alternate times loving and sexual, assertive and violent, Inanna was able to demolish all opposition. It is a sobering version of the goddess, more like the Hindu goddess Kali, with her fiery eyes and garland of human heads, than any compassionate force. Inanna does not seem to have compassion even though she was the epitome of sexual love. She was a goddess capable of striking fear, particularly into men; an unhinged, violent, chaotic power of the creative earth/female, uncontrollable, unpredictable, capable of sweeping mere mortals to their death.

Meador wrote, "Inanna is an unsubdued, multifaceted, energetic female force. She is raw energy bursting for expression. She is raw libidinous vitality," expressed through four avenues: warrior, priestess, lover and androgyne. "There is no hint here of the Christian concept of womanhood." [42]

No male, whether human or divine, could dominate her, and the one man who did take advantage of her paid dearly. In a myth known as *Inanna and Šu-kale-tuda*, a young gardener violates the goddess as she lies sleeping under a tree. When the goddess awakes, she sees what has been done to her sacred vulva and sets out on a ferocious search for the man. Unable to find his name or whereabouts from local residents, Inanna turns the rivers red with her blood, threatening death to everyone until finally one of the gods in Sumer reveals the man's location. Inanna kills the rapist.

But this is far more than a simple story of rape. The tree under which Inanna sleeps is the "Tree of Life," planted by the god of fresh waters. Moreover, Inanna wears a loincloth across her thighs that weaves together seven cosmic powers—a cloth that the young man removes in order to penetrate her. In addition, the "gardener" has just uprooted the plants he was tending, thereby doing violence to the earth as well.

When scholar and poet Judy Grahn interpreted the ancient hymn, she called it a "myth of ecofeminism,"[43] in which the "power of women's bodies (is) magnified as powers of nature." Grahn writes: "By knitting the imagery together, the (Sumerian) poet ties together the two transgressions, sexual and ecological—a man who would carelessly transgress the Land would carelessly transgress the person of the Woman as well. The belt across Inanna's loins contains the laws or orders of nature; the implication is that her vulva holds things together for the world of Sumer.

"The myth tells us through the character of Inanna that when nature is not approached with love and respect, with mindfulness, and with consciousness of self, the result is chaos for us, and not just death, but also disappearance, and disconnection."

Few goddess myths could be more applicable to our modern problems than this one. The sin is represented as rape of a goddess, but in larger context, it is a crime against the natural world and its creative powers. We are reminded that nature carries both creative and destructive powers, with no guarantees of goodness.

AN ALL-ENCOMPASSING DEITY

Inanna is so multifaceted and paradoxical that virtually no aspect of life escapes her grasp. This is particularly true as she gathers by hook or by crook the powers of the other gods, generating a long list of qualities and principles (named the **me**; pronounced "*may*") over which she exercises control. On an early journey to the god of wisdom, Enki, the young goddess accepts an invitation to drink with him—a mistake on his part. Enki gets thoroughly drunk and impulsively offers Inanna his powers. (She had previously complained to him about not having any "*me*.")

Inanna quickly absconds with the gift. Once sober, the older god tries to retrieve his offering, but she will not give it back. Inanna escapes the demons he throws at her until she reaches the safety of her temple and from then on, she holds sway over heaven and earth, nature and civilization both.

"We have nothing in the western pantheons of goddesses that even approaches her variety and dominion," wrote Meador. "Inanna emerges as an all-encompassing, over-arching (sic) deity, even an attempt at a unitary vision."[44]

How do we, as modern women, hold this goddess? Not a mother, she seemed to lack nurturing instincts. (There was another, less well-known Mesopotamian goddess for this role). She fought and defeated her opponents as a man would, with courage. "She does not hesitate to challenge any obstacle," and exhibits an "exuberant zest, a joyful, voracious appetite for life."

"If this zest for life were Inanna's only mode of being a warrior, it would not be difficult for the modern woman to follow," says Meador. "Her hands-on-hips, legs-planted stand fits today's model of the assertive woman." But in her warrior myths, Inanna assumes much darker proportions and becomes "the random destructiveness of natural disaster as well as the ravenous goddess of death."[45]

Inanna is nature unbound, taking us back (or forward) to a time when the gods of Abraham did not have dominion over the natural world. To the Sumerians she was a divine force in the material world and in her stories we see the paradoxes we all live with—the alternating blessings and curses, the darkness and light, the goodness and evil, the reality we cope with every day while hoping for the best.

Inanna combats any attempt to call into question the primacy of nature as the body of the goddess. In one of the three poems interpreted by Meador, Enheduanna shows her goddess becoming enraged by the effort of a sacred mountain, named Ebih, to set up a paradise on its flanks, a peaceable kingdom where trees always bear fruit and lions lie down with lambs. This move away from nature into an idealized realm was not permissible to her. The goddess strikes:

> *"My Queen batters the mountain*
> *plants her heels hard*
> *rubs dagger's edge on a whet stone*
>
> *grabs Ebih by the neck*
> *as she would a sheaf of rushes*
>
> *in ear-splitting waves*
> *her shrill cries pierce*
> *Ebih's failing heart*
>
> *with stones from its own slopes*
> *she pelts   she pounds*
> *thud dub   thud dub*
> *storms of stones crack its sides*
>
> *damp and writhing snakes*
> *tangled in branches*
> *drop at her drear bidding*
> *spitting deadly venom*

and her tongue's poison
hurls a green-wilting curse
over forest and fruit-bearing trees

She shows no mercy
to its plant rows
a parching drought she blows
dust dry air in her pitiless wake
gusts over stems of verdant growth
not a moist drop stays

in the bent and withered grass
she strikes fires
flames cut the sky to the boundary stones
flames dance in the smoke stained air
spread at a glance from the queen's glare

holy Inanna
fresh faced, fearless
vigor of a young man commanding

wrestles the mountain to its knees
stands the victor at its base [46]

In the book's longest poem, "Lady of Largest Heart," Inanna

…soaks her mace
in blood and gore
smashes heads
butchers prey
with eater-ax and
bloodied spear
all day
these evil blades
the warrior flings

pours blood on offerings
so who she feeds
dines on death...

As Meador confronted the raw words presented by the translations: "ax," "smashes heads," "serves up death," "blood," "tears to pieces," she wrote, "Inanna's bloody appetite and terrorizing revenge made me shudder. In verse after verse, Enheduanna spat out the punishment this vindictive goddess inflicted on her worshippers."[47]

But as the full poetry took shape, Meador, a Jungian analyst, began to see the cycles of light and dark, the alternating beauty and calm order, mixed with terrifying, jumbled disorder that make up our everyday experience as human beings in a mysterious world of matter.

What is true about life and divinity? We don't know. Why are we subjected to this ebb and flow of mind-bending pain and blessed contentment? It's the natural order. There lies Gaia, earth-life. You cannot resolve it, or change it, or think it away, or construct a secure sanctuary against darkness and destruction. The dark pieces belong to us too. And we learn to live with them, if we learn to live at all. The original female deity represented nature in its full reality—not just creation or pregnancy, but destruction and death.

This is the dark side of female divinity, the side that was repressed by monotheistic male gods—the underworld with its witches, the fearsome power of earthquake, fire and flood, once personified as female deities that humans worshipped in the hope they could appease death and destruction. Some 600–1,000 years after this period, Abraham would be born in Ur, the same city where Enheduanna worshipped Inanna, later known as "Ishtar" in Semitic manifestations, and "Astarte." Stories of the Garden of Eden would reinvent human origins and give the male gender dominion over nature and over women.

Inanna is far more aggressive and less nurturing than was Gimbutas's Great Goddess from the earlier Neolithic period.

Basing her vision on the archaeology of the Stone Age before villages were threatened by invasion, Gimbutas saw a primarily peaceful life, marked by rhythmic cycles of birth and death. Carnivorous birds such as ravens were depicted with female traits, but this occurred in the context of defleshing dead bodies. And there was no death without regeneration. At least, that's what Gimbutas said, based on her reading of the archaeology. Without writing, we don't really know what belief systems came with the Great Goddess.

By contrast, Enheduanna was the daughter of King Sargon of Agade, the first imperialist in history who brought all of Mesopotamia under his rule before branching out into Anatolia and much of the rest of the known world. She grew up with stories of conquest and must have been influenced by the growing power, war and aggression unleashed by emerging states, as well as by the evolution of kings and social hierarchy. Her father made her high priestess at the temple in Ur, a position from which she gradually elevated Inanna to dominance.

But patriarchy was on the move. Enheduanna had to fight a threat by male relatives who wanted to depose her and institute the divine right of kings. She was physically thrown out of her temple at one time, although she later regained it. Perhaps her depiction of the outright aggressiveness of her goddess, Inanna, was influenced by these life events. We will never know.

I am not alone among humans in needing something to mitigate the reality Inanna represented. I can't live with nature unbound, the "red in tooth and claw" kind, and if a belief in gods and goddesses doesn't bring relief, what will? For me, that something is human love and compassion. I believe that humans have evolved to express the binding forces of the universe through our capacity to love and care for each other, over which—and this is the important point—we have control. It is by choice that we have compassion, by choice that we love each other, by choice that we learn to stop the violence. We provide the pity in the natural world, which otherwise may not help us when we need it.

The goddess we know from the earliest days of the written record represented unmitigated reality, which is to say the alternately wonderful and horrifying world of constant change. She may be beautiful, but she is also too terrifying to resurrect without the touch of human compassion. She carries death and destruction, as well as life and regeneration in the patterns of an unplanned wilderness. You can't eat that for breakfast.

Inanna brings no reliable healing for human pain. For that, we need the compassion of other human beings to transform reality with human caring. We need the message of Christ or the Buddha. Without compassion, we are left as on a darkling plain, in a world of beauty and destruction that seems to change in disregard for our welfare.

If I were a Christian, I might say we need Christ's love. But I'm not Christian anymore. Christ promised too much. For me, Christian belief splits the metaphysical realm into heaven and hell. Jesus represents only good, while darkness belongs to the Devil. Some say that if you believe in Him, you don't suffer anymore. But that doesn't work for me. I can't accept a duality of good and evil. Nor can I put faith in a divine personage, whether Christ or some other prophet. The only way to help our suffering, I believe, is to care for each other. "Karuna," the ancient Pali word for compassion, is the desire to help when you see someone or something hurting. It also means "love" in the largest universal sense of that word. Karuna is the core of Buddha's teachings.

I end this chapter with a poem by Rick Fields, published in a book of Buddhist essays.[48] The poem fell into my hands in 2017 and helped me along this journey of exploration. Notice that the two eyes of the goddess, as she meets Buddha, are "fathomless pits of space," while a third eye is a "ring of fire."

The Very Short Sutra on the Meeting of the Buddha and the Goddess

Thus I have made up:
           Once the Buddha was walking along the
forest path in the Oak Grove at Ojai, walking without
arriving anywhere
or having any thought of arriving or not arriving

and lotuses shining with the morning dew
miraculously appeared under every step
soft as silk beneath the toes of the Buddha

When suddenly, out of the turquoise sky,
dancing in front of his half-shut inward-looking
eyes, shimmering like a rainbow
or a spider's web
transparent as the dew on a lotus flower,

—the Goddess appeared quivering
like a hummingbird in the air before him

She, for she was surely a she
as the Buddha could clearly see
with his eye of discriminating awareness wisdom,

was mostly red in color
though when the light shifted
she flashed like a rainbow.

She was naked except
for the usual flower ornaments
Goddesses wear

Her long hair
was deep blue, her two eyes fathomless pits of space
and her third eye a bloodshot
ring of fire.

The Buddha folded his hands together
and greeted the Goddess thus:

"O Goddess, why are you blocking my path.
Before I saw you I was happily going nowhere.
Now I'm not sure where to go."

"You can go around me,"
said the Goddess, twirling on her heels like a bird
darting away,
but just a little way away,
"or you can come after me.
This is my forest too,
you can't pretend I'm not here."

With that the Buddha sat
          supple as a snake
          solid as a rock
beneath a Bo tree
          that sprang full-leaved
          to shade him.

"Perhaps we should have a chat,"
he said.
"After years of arduous practice
at the time of the morning star
I penetrated reality, and now..."

"Not so fast, Buddha.
I *am* reality.

The Earth stood still,
the oceans paused,

the wind itself listened
—a thousand arhats, bodhisattvas, and dakinis
magically appeared to hear
what would happen in the conversation.

"I know I take my life in my hands."
said the Buddha.
"But I am known as the Fearless One
—so here goes."

And he and the Goddess
without further words
exchanged glances.

Light rays like sunbeams
shot forth
so bright that even
Sariputra, the All-Seeing One,
had to turn away.

And then they exchanged thoughts
and the illumination was as bright as a diamond candle.

And then they exchanged mind
And there was a great silence as vast as the universe
that contains everything

And then they exchanged bodies
And clothes

And the Buddha arose
as the Goddess
and the Goddess
arose as the Buddha

and so on back and forth
for a hundred thousand hundred thousand kalpas.

If you meet the Buddha
you meet the Goddess.
If you meet the Goddess
you meet the Buddha.

Not only that. This:
The Buddha is the Goddess,
the Goddess is the Buddha.

And not only that. This:
The Buddha is emptiness
the Goddess is bliss,
the Goddess is emptiness
the Buddha is bliss.

And that is what
and what-not you are
It's true.

So here comes the mantra of the Goddess and the Buddha, the
unsurpassed non-dual mantra. Just to say this mantra, just to hear
this mantra once, just to hear one word of this mantra once makes
everything the way it truly is: OK.

So here it is:

> Earth-walker/sky-walker
>> Hey, silent one, Hey, great talker
> Not two/Not one
>> Not separate/Not apart
> This is the heart
>> Bliss is emptiness
>> Emptiness is bliss
> Be your breath, Ah
> Smile, Hey
> And relax, Ho

And remember this: You can't miss.

> —*By Rick Fields*

MY QUESTION: If the Buddha gives the Goddess compassion, what does the Goddess give the Buddha?

HER ANSWER: An embodied mind and sex to make your head spin.

NINE

MODERN VILLAGES

We stood in a circle under the old oak tree on a moonlit solstice night in 1999, passing around glasses of champagne on a silver tray to toast the new year and the new millennium. The tree was 200 years old and the full Super Moon was enormous, as close to earth that year as it ever comes. There were about twenty-five of us—men, women and children of all ages—standing on the open, grassy two acres of land that was the site of our future homes. We danced a bit; we toasted each other and the new adventure we had started. In two years, we would all move onto that piece of land, newly built for a community of thirty-two households. It would be our own place, managed and governed by us through consensus of the whole. We had only a dim idea of what that meant.

National commentators periodically lament the loss of community in modern life. We don't know each other anymore. We pass by neighbors with no more than "hello," if that. Every technological advance takes us further away from personal engagement. Soon, they say, we will all be walking around in a virtual reality—the real one unseen.

I wanted to go in the other direction. Twenty years earlier I had pledged to myself that I would find an environment that nurtured me. I did not intend to be lonely the rest of my life. This meant more than just finding a partner; I wanted to reconstruct a sense of community as I had known it in my youth in Sacramento, the loss of which was so painful to me.

I remember thinking in Philadelphia, in those lonely years after I left Don, that if we humans had evolved to live in small social groups, what were we—what was I—doing living cooped up alone in separate apartments with tenuous personal attachments and too much media? Society had evolved to the point where it made some people rich and other people sick. One day I kicked at the wall with my boot and put a hole through it. The wall happened to be cardboard-thin under the stairs and I stood in shock looking at the results of my fury. The black hole gaped back at me. I stood at the window contemplating my options then and pledged that I would find surroundings that would nurture my well-being. The fault lay not in myself but in the environment.

Part of my solution lay in coming back to California where I had strong ties. Janet and her husband, Loren, were fun companions. We often camped together in their pop-up tent trailer, spending gorgeous winters in Yosemite, with New Year's brunch at the Ahwahnee Hotel. We hiked the Kalalau Trail on Kauai in Hawaii, which at times seemed to threaten the unwary with a 1,000-foot drop into the Pacific. The threat was underlined by a storage attendant who, in taking our baggage, asked for a forwarding address.

"Why do you need that?" we asked.

"Well, sometimes," she answered, "people don't come back."

It was healing to reconnect with family. But to make my life stable and secure for the next fifty years (I expect to live past 100, as my mother and aunts have done), I needed my own home. That began for me with the solstice ritual in 1999—the beginning of a new and healthy environment. Nineteen years later, I can say that living in the vicinity of four dozen neighbors who know me has anchored my life in ways I could not have dreamed of.

Our place—seven condo buildings and a common house on an acre and a half of land—was built by two architects, Kathryn McCamant and Charles Durrett—"Chuck and Katie" to those who know them. A visionary couple who brought their dream of cohousing from Denmark, their book describing a new vision of living together in community, first published in 1988,[49] has been called by *The New York Times* a "bible" of the movement.

Chuck and Katie's vision of changing America, one neighborhood at a time, is focused on building not just houses but neighborhoods where residents know each other and govern together. There would be a central commons with cars parked on the periphery. There would be a common house where we could gather for meals, hold meetings and celebrations and host guests. There would be kitchens in the front of our thirty-two households where we would see our neighbors pass by, with living rooms and bedrooms in the back for more private encounters. There would be training sessions so we could learn how to make decisions without hierarchy or authority imposed from the outside. Direct democracy it was. Whoever heard of that?

Cohousing is and was a radical re-envisioning of community life in America. Since the night I first heard them in the late '80s, Chuck and Katie have built about seventy of these communities throughout the country, including my own. Other builders have brought the total to more than 150 cohousing communities in the past three decades.

I have never regretted for a moment this choice of life and feel a deep gratitude toward Chuck and Katie for making it possible. When I first laid eyes on my beautiful condo apartment with its nine-foot ceilings, empty and waiting for me, I was swept with awareness: Home at last! I had been in flight for most of my life and now had landed. Let the new life begin.

At first, we lived with hierarchy. While our houses were being constructed, the builders and a select few of our group made most of the decisions. The physical plant had to be created quickly; you couldn't debate every nail and stud. As individuals, we had some input on the way our houses were designed, but for the most part, we only watched while the whole thing materialized before our eyes. Then, the day came when the builders left. We looked at each other. We were alone. It was just us, no authority.

"What do we do now?" a neighbor asked with wonder. No one answered. Perhaps we all felt the same way, like children who are suddenly adults with no one around to direct the action. So, how *do* you run a community of some fifty adults, a dozen children and property worth about $2 million? We were going to maintain the property ourselves without hired managers. Each household elected a member to the board of directors so there was no overarching, separate board. Without a hierarchy and with no one to blame but ourselves, we had to quickly establish a neighborhood government of some sort.

Over the next few months, we tentatively began to construct a system based on committees that would manage our physical and financial business. (We own the property in common but houses are privately owned.) We would also elect officers, but they would have no more power than any other committee and all would be subject to group consensus achieved through monthly meetings.

One of the first things we noticed was that group consensus empowered us as individuals. Any one of us could stop an entire decision with one vote, one blocking vote. I remember the day I realized that my opinion mattered—a strange realization in modern life where we regularly swallow tons of distressing news and know that our vote is just one of millions; individually we have very little chance of changing anything. But here, every voice mattered. Paradoxically that meant that except for the occasional outlier, no one wanted to be a problem. The natural tendency to suppress dissent in order to be socially acceptable showed itself as "group think." People tended to go along with prevailing opinion without disclosing honest feelings.

Group think produces terrible decisions. The wisdom of the collective is not apparent when people are trying to fit in. I remember nights when I feared being ostracized because I had an unpopular opinion on some community matter. I was scared of being socially isolated—a fear no doubt bred into our genes from millions of years living in small bands of human beings.

So we made a deliberate decision: as a policy we would support lone dissenters, even when it meant months of living in the "groan zone," our term for the lengthy process of working out differences. The groaning comes when you face another meeting on a subject—especially those concerning money—that you really don't want to talk about anymore. Over time, when it seemed as though the community would splinter over some issue, we would suddenly realize, "Oh, yeah. We're in the groan zone. It will pass."

Another early discovery came from the process of bumping up against each other with ingrained habits of sarcasm, suspicion, defensiveness, uncharitable gossiping and rapid-fire temper blowups. The list goes on. I had believed I was a nice, empathetic woman. But I had not been tested in a real bonded community where I learned about myself—and my subtle aggressions—more deeply. Neighbors were honest with me (imagine that!) but accepting. I became anchored as an individual in a network of people I saw every day. A friend recalled that before cohousing she knew only one neighbor well enough to greet when she left her house. Now she sees three people she loves when she walks out the door. She may also see someone she's learned to tolerate, but that's okay too.

In a normal suburban neighborhood, any disagreement may cause permanent disruption; you never talk to one another again. In my neighborhood, you pass by each other all day, eat together several times a week and govern together. You will not become close friends with everyone, but you need to be civil.

Conflict in a bonded neighborhood can be tough. I don't mean to minimize that. You own your house. If fighting becomes intractable, it can take years to decide to leave and actually make the move. In the meantime, many people suffer. One year, when confronted with distressing internal dissension, we decided to hire some trainers in the business of nonviolent communication. No one had to take the training, yet two-thirds of us voluntarily signed up to learn how to speak to each other with more understanding. It was a good thing. We also have hired an expert in community process to help us develop fair methods of reaching a vote if consensus does not work.

I write this kind of detail because I want to be explicit about my worldview and its source. And because I believe that prehistoric people possessed more advanced social behavior than we have today because they lived in small bonded communities.

Evolution provided us with marvelous social capacity—no other species of ape could last through a morning on the New York subway without committing mayhem. But we do not develop these skills to a high degree when we live in neighborhoods that lack meaningful contact among households. It's possible that in modern American life, we all tend to be on the aggressive, self-centered side compared to hunter-gatherers. But our capacity is so much greater than what we see in our lives today.

In the movie *Wonder Woman*, the heroine challenges the nasty view of the human race promulgated by her arch-enemy Ares, the god of war. Wonder Woman says, "They are all that you say, but so much more."

We are worth saving.

When commentators talk about "tribal behavior" in criticizing contemporary divisions in American society, they do an injustice to tribal people, most of whom dealt with intractable conflict by walking away and avoiding each other. Anyone who lives in small communities knows this is true. No question, there were patriarchal groups who regularly fought each other and maintained strict boundaries around their territory. But this is not how most hunting and gathering groups lived their lives throughout the millennia, before technological advance and patriarchy altered social systems across the globe.

Nor is it the way we lived before modern capitalism tore our communities apart and substituted electronic media for human contact. Stripped of cultural memory of what it was like to live in a neighborhood where everyone knew each other, we no longer understand this kind of relationship.

But cohousing visionary Chuck Durrett remembers. In a recent interview with me, he remembered having "grown up in a small town in northern California. I knew the difference," he said, "between a post-World War II suburb and a high-functioning neighborhood. He recalled that one day, as a student in Denmark, he was walking down the street to the train station when he "noticed an extraordinary neighborhood. There was a cluster of houses where people had brought together picnic tables. They were gardening together and coming and going to a building where apparently nobody lived but everyone entered. I stopped and said to myself, 'What the heck is going on here?'"

A few years later, now married to Katie, the two went back to Denmark for a year to study the innovative housing development the Danes called "living communities." Back in the US, they started a movement that they named "cohousing," with the mission, as expressed on a bumper sticker, of "Changing the World, One Neighborhood at a Time."

Building a community with cars on the outside and a central commons is important, but not the critical element. "This is about the process," said Chuck. "It's about knowing that if I cooperate with my neighbor, we're going to make a smarter decision or find a smarter tool—every time."

I can validate that from my nineteen years in cohousing, during which time we have discovered the wisdom of the crowd (as long as we support dissent). Cohousing is not family. It's something different. We don't raise children together. Some families with small children who moved here eagerly anticipated getting a tribe of new "grandmothers." But they soon found that we older women were not particularly available as babysitters. We wanted to create a new, vibrant community and there was much to learn, much to try out. This was no small adventure; it took a lot of time and it still does.

Parents have a kids committee and they make the rules for children on the property, which other adults may help implement, but normally the community as a whole relates to children by providing protected space to play in and amused neighbors who appreciate their bugs and spiders, drawings and performances.

Nor do we provide in-home care for each other. In times of medical need, we bring daily meals, along with visits and rides to the doctor, but if you've just had surgery, you have to hire a caregiver. (Cohousing communities vary a great deal; I'm only talking about my own.)

Cohousing is also not a commune. We don't share private economic resources, though neighbors may lend each other money. The old-style commune where people farmed together and lived cooperatively is far more integrated than my own. Here, we each own our fully equipped houses or condos, bought at market rate under established state law for private residences. You can, if you wish, isolate yourself in complete privacy within your four walls, but then, why would you live here if not to join in the soul-connecting events of community life?

Jay was one of our founding members, among the first five to join this project and an absolute advocate of cohousing. He never stopped singing its praises. Then he fell ill with cancer and was hospitalized. Knowing he did not have long to live, we organized a banquet for him to celebrate his life, expecting that he could return in time to hear our stories and feel the love.

Our dining room was filled as evening fell and we waited. And waited. Finally we began dinner without him as an ambulance drew up outside. Medics lowered Jay onto a gurney. We flooded outdoors, lining up along both sides of the pathway that crosses our commons, each of us carrying a candle that lit the gathering darkness with fifty points of light. I cannot forget the gurney rolling up the path between us with Jay under a blanket, unconscious. He never woke up again. We sang anyway, a song written by Joanne, one of our members, called "This Place." I like to think that with some part of his mind he heard us welcome him home.

> Come into this place of peace, let its
>   silence heal your spirit
> Come into the place of memory, let its
>   history warm your soul
> Let this place move and change you.
>   Oh this place will re-arrange you!
> Let this place be changed because of you.
>   Welcome Home.

Come into this place of children, let the
    laughter lift your day
Come into this place of friendship, let a
    handshake warm your heart
Let this place move and change you.
    Oh this place will re-arrange you!
Let this place be changed because of you.
    Welcome Home.

Come in with hurt and anger, and reach
    down deep inside
You know at least one neighbor will listen
    and confide
Let this place move and change you.
    Oh this place will re-arrange you!
Let this place be changed because of you.
    Welcome Home.

When another elder who helped start the community died a
few years later, we held space for him for three days during hospice,
filing in by twos and threes to sit by his bedside. I was caught, as
were others, by a special state of mind, a sense of a shared sacred
consciousness that was not apparent to me until it was over and I
opened to the outside world again.

As we age in this neighborhood, people have wondered how the
community will carry on without the experienced work of the elder
women (one younger woman called us "matriarchs"). Not all of the
elders are women, but it's a high percentage. The three deaths in the
community have all been men. I think we have the answer now.

There's been a generational shift in the past two years with
lots of younger people moving in to fill spaces left by those who
moved after their children went off to college. The new people,
including many men, have stepped up with complete willingness
to carry forth this way of life. They plan to raise their children

here. The young energy rises through community dances and celebrations of all sorts. We will continue. And it does not depend on
any one of us alone. Each of us carries only a piece of the whole,
as represented by our "tie-in" ceremony. When we welcome new
residents, we drag out our fabric rope made out of separate pieces
of fabric from each household, and stand in a circle, singing as we
add the new pieces to the ones that bear our names.

It may seem romantic to think this modern village is like
those built thousands of years ago as humans first settled down
on the land, but we share some important features with ancient
villages. We eat together several times a week, a critical element
of social cohesion. To the people of Çatalhöyük, 9,000 years ago,
eating groups formed the basis of social groups as found in the
remains of burials.

Secondly, elder women are important to the governing process
in cohousing, as they were in egalitarian societies of record and
probably those of prehistory as well. And decisions are made by
consensus in such groups.

There is one important feature we do not share, however—
religion. Indigenous egalitarian groups normally have a female
founder or divine spirit. In my community, we don't have a
common religious or political philosophy, although some intentional communities do. Most of my neighbors are, like me, liberal
environmentalists but that is a product of our location and time,
not the selection process.

But are we really like the ancient towns that predated patriarchal organization and archaic cities? Did people govern themselves
by consensus? Were men and women ever equal as leaders and
sacred symbols?

For the sake of clarity, I am distinguishing between male-dominant cultures, which in this memoir refer to small pre-western
tribal societies, and patriarchy. Patriarchy describes a larger system
that arose with warfare and imperialism during the Bronze Age.
I use this term to refer to both male domination and social stratification. It is prone to economic expansion, a continuation of

the pattern begun in early archaic states with kings and armies. Relatively few people, those at the top (primarily men) reap its benefits. It is kept in place by fear of outside threats. Both systems condition men to be tough, with some level of disrespect for the "opposite" sex.

In egalitarian cultures, women did not choose to dominate men, if that were even possible. Unlike men—who become hyper-aggressive in a cultural process that shapes their psychology so that they will risk their lives—the female, giver of new life, never was used that way. Nor have women controlled men in the cultures where they held economic and religious authority.

A matriarchy (or egalitarian pattern), as it turns out, is a completely different system or set of systems. I learned a long time ago from the established canon in anthropology that no culture ever created a matriarchy—meaning a female version of patriarchy. That remains true in all the examples I could find. But the women in these egalitarian cultures did have power. They shared the roles and benefits of public life that conferred respect. They had economic strength and a voice in decisions not limited to maternal functions. And they were safe from sexual abuse; males learned from childhood to honor females. Rape was nonexistent.

Egalitarian cultures offer us a fundamentally different and more peaceful world than we have seen from the common male-dominated view of society. A prominent advocate of this perspective, anthropologist Eleanor Leacock, has written that during the millions of years of human evolution as hunters and gatherers, most cultures were egalitarian, not ordinarily given to violent conflict. They would decamp in the night rather than fight. Avoiding each other was vastly preferred to murder and mayhem when one lived in small communities of thirty to fifty individuals.

"Societies that lived by gathering and by hunting (and fishing) were cooperative. People shared food and thought of greed and selfishness much as we might think of mentally ill or criminal behavior. People made and valued fine possessions, but as much to give away as to keep," Leacock wrote.[50] She surmised that they were less aggressive than people today because they needed each other more.

More recent studies support Leacock's conclusion[51] that hunters and gatherers were gender-equal. But what happened when humans settled down in permanent towns during the agricultural revolution?

For that, I turn to one of the oldest towns on Earth: Çatalhöyük, located in Anatolia, the ancient territory in central Turkey that rings with the haunting sounds of an unbelievably distant past. Anatolia and nearby Levant are the places where virtually all of the oldest sources of Middle Eastern and Indo-European culture flourished.

One of the major towns of the Neolithic, Çatalhöyük stands out for its long existence without warfare. At 9,000 years old, it is one of the first towns in the evolution of the human species. Men and women lived there for almost 2,000 years without violence and they have something to tell us: Egalitarianism is linked with a more peaceful world.

TEN

EGALITARIAN CULTURES

ÇATALHÖYÜK: OF URBAN ORIGINS

It was a cold day in January 2018 as I drove from my home in the San Francisco East Bay to interview Stanford archaeologist Ian Hodder, leader of an international group of specialists at Çatalhöyük for more than twenty years. He received me graciously in his stone-walled office, but I could see from his eyes that he was wary. Hodder has spent years explaining to women why he doesn't "see" goddesses in Çatalhöyük. I was hardly the first to wonder how he came to interpret a mysterious wall sculpture at Çatalhöyük as a "bear" when others saw it as a "goddess." That change shook the study of goddess cultures. But, before getting to difficult material, I wanted to know about egalitarian culture at this very ancient site.

"This was an egalitarian society," said Hodder. "Whether you were a man or woman didn't seem to have been relevant to social standing or position." Both genders carried out many roles and positions, from making tools to baking and heading a household," he said.

"Depictions of feasting rituals imply that men dominated in this realm. But we can discern no sign that they had an overarching influence on other areas of life."[52]

The largest settlement of prehistoric people known from the early days of the Agricultural Revolution, Çatalhöyük dates from about 7,000 BCE. About 8,000 people lived there over a period of more than 1,500 years with no evidence of warfare, and few signs of violence of any sort. They were immersed in the natural world, not yet separated by greed or hierarchy from the earth that gave them life, accepting death as part of a natural cycle.

"They came together to link into a dense network," said Hodder. He described a community life that was not particularly organized upon the basis of conjugal families: "People were tied together; any individual could call upon help from many."

The town was densely packed with houses right up against each other (although they didn't share walls; inches separated the houses). People apparently moved around on the rooftops because there were no streets, not even room for a street. They climbed down into their dwellings by ladder from the roof. Nor did related family members necessarily live together. They may have slept together—that is unknown—but they were not buried together. Archaeological evidence indicates that the people who were buried together were those that shared meals over their lifetimes, and if their teeth are a sufficient indication of genetic relatedness, they were not close relatives.

"These groups constructed history out of their events, but they were obviously not one family," said Hodder. "In fact, it's possible to argue that at Çatalhöyük you wouldn't even know who you were genetically related to."

In a wider context, political and social organization of Çatalhöyük lacked a central hierarchy or wealth differences among people. Some houses were larger than others, but they did not contain any more material—no extra decorations, no additional storage. Men and women did similar things. They ate the same food; they both carried out domestic tasks. Not only were there no status differences between men and women, but also no evidence among individuals at large, no signs of wealth accumulation or hierarchy among the different groups. Hodder confessed that he does not know how that was done. Puzzled, he said, "How is it possible for so many people to live together in such a collective way? You would think they needed a central hierarchy."

He was not particularly positive about this arrangement, preferring to label it "aggressively" egalitarian. In the interview, I asked him what the modifier meant. Did he mean to say the equality was coerced or forced?

"I don't have any evidence that it was directly coerced. But I'm including the notion of consensus [under the umbrella of "coercion"]. I'm accepting that there was a social consensus that imposed these limits. My assumption is that there would be people who would want to accumulate wealth."

"But," I countered, "equality isn't necessarily based on force; it may arise through shared community values."

"You're right," he replied. "I can't say there was physical coercion, but I assume there was some sort of constraint placed on people." In the upper layers of the site representing later periods at Çatalhöyük (6,000 BCE), the level of equality changes and certain houses become ritually and economically dominant, he said.

Others have had a different view of the lack of visible stratification and leadership at Çatalhöyük. Historian Anne Barstow, known for her writings on earlier excavations at the site, has said that the mystery lies in the lack of our expected roles for men. Without a hierarchy or a military, positions of power that men usually hold did not exist. But women exercised certain kinds of power, based on their control of agriculture. From this economic base, they created a religion "devoted to the preservation of life in all forms," Barstow wrote[53] in an essay in *The Book of the Goddess, Past and Present.*

In spite of his use of loaded qualifiers for "egalitarian," the story Hodder had to tell about the way these people lived their lives was quite wonderful. I've quoted from our interview some of his descriptions below.

The town seems to have been divided into eating groups, people who came together from different houses and stayed together over generations, yet were not genetically related to each other.

"We call them history houses," Hodder said. "They're not a neighborhood. They're buildings with more burials and ritual symbolism." He explained that the houses seem to bring together individual histories so that "the dead, the ancestors and much of the ritual paraphernalia is handed down generation to generation."

Such generational transmission seems strange in a modern context because it was not based on genetic families — or rather not limited to genetic ties, but included many apparently unrelated individuals.

"The people are amassing histories, not only of families, but of feasts in the past and balls and things they were associated with," Hodder told me. "They kept these things in the history houses and handed them down through time." Such eating groups had continuity over centuries.

In addition, Hodder said Çatalhöyük residents had other groups based on particular symbols, "clans, perhaps a bear clan, or a leopard clan," as well as groups for medicine and hunting societies. Then there were exchange groups relating to obsidian and ceramic production.

"In my view, Çatalhöyük is a web in that any particular individual can say 'I'm a member of this history house, and a member of that clan and this extended exchange group,'" Hodder said, noting that we no longer have "complex overlapping social groups to this extent. It's a fantastic model," he said.

History houses were highly significant as places where residents ceremonially buried the skulls of important ancestors under the foundation stones: "Heads got removed from individuals and circulated over a period of time," Hodder told me.

"These were very significant ancestors, which were kept 'alive' over the centuries. There were as many women as there were men. They were founders in a sense."

As in many egalitarian societies, gender equality among the founders came with equality among the living.

Hodder described the people of Çatalhöyük as very "rule-bound," in that excavators would always find the same things in the same places through generations of building. They apparently were strongly oriented toward the four directions, so that hearth and sleeping areas, for instance, were always in the same places. Also, they never let dogs into their houses, among other rules. And they did not amass wealth; did not have different economic strata.

Paradoxically, he added that Çatalhöyük residents were very individualistic, more so than are people today, at least as judged by their artistic production and burial practices, which included one individual buried with weasel scat.

"We live in a society where we are supposed to be individualistic, but in fact we're not. Çatalhöyük is the opposite of this. Strong rules. But people were allowed to do strange things," said Hodder.

The work at Çatalhöyük for the last twenty-five years has completely upended earlier interpretations that this was a "goddess" society where people worshipped the sacred female.

That story was set in motion by James Mellaart, whose work I first heard about in the 1970s with such powerful emotional effect. Since then, the deconstruction of Mellaart's findings has been central to the wholesale takedown of a Neolithic goddess in anthropological studies.

But if Hodder hasn't "seen" any goddess figures at Çatalhöyük, he did see gender equality in the use of skulls as cultural founders. His observations square with findings in many egalitarian societies where a female "founder" can be just as important as a deity, standing in as central actor in a sacred story of cultural origins. Whether they call her a goddess or a founder, indigenous people may pass down these stories through rituals that are enacted over and over again, creating real-life authority for women in a template of sacred authority.

THE IROQUOIS: AMERICA'S ORIGINAL DEMOCRACY

The Iroquois once defeated the French in a battle that so humiliated the French they could never admit who beat them. It happened during the seventeenth century near Lake Ontario at a place called Fort Frontenac. During a series of battles called the Beaver Wars, the French tricked the Iroquois into attending a fake peace council where they took all the native attendees prisoner, and sent them off to Europe as galley slaves.

Apparently they believed that without leadership, the Iroquois's ability to fight would collapse. What they didn't know was that at home, the Iroquois had a parallel authority structure headed by a woman, the Clan Mother. The Women's Council was traditionally in charge of appointing warriors and declaring war, although they did not ordinarily fight. In this case, however, the women took up weapons along with newly enlisted men and launched a full-out attack against the French, driving them out of Fort Frontenac while also capturing a load of European munitions. It was a woman who commanded the rout, which neither the French at the time, nor subsequent historians, have ever admitted.

This story is told by Iroquois scholar Barbara Alice Mann in her opus on female power among the Haudenosaunee,[54] an in-depth reconstruction of the authority wielded by women in the six-nation League. Digging into a mountain of patriarchal-themed writing by Western scholars over four centuries, Mann was able to uncover the stunning degree of female empowerment in Iroquois culture. These powers, known to early feminists, substantially influenced the 1848 convention in Seneca Falls, NY, where American women called for an end to Western male dominance.

Records of the seventeenth and eighteenth centuries demonstrate that newly arrived Europeans and Iroquois interacted on a daily basis. Some have claimed that early Americans learned democratic processes from the Iroquois, leading to the US Constitution. Others challenge such conclusions. What is more certain is the degree to which European-American women were affected. Organizers of the 1848 convention, including Elizabeth Cady Stanton, were quite familiar with the Iroquois model, and in some cases, even shared relations with the Native Americans. Their equality served as an inspiration from the earliest days of feminism.

"They believed women's liberation was possible because they knew liberated women, women who possessed rights beyond their wildest imagination: Haudenosaunee women," said Sally Roesch Wagner in her history of the influence exercised by Iroquoian women on early feminists.[55]

Iroquois women appointed chiefs, farmed the land (which they inherited through mothers) and distributed all the material goods. The Iroquois did not see land as owned by anyone, but it was farmed and managed by women, who grew most of the food. Men hunted. Men also held official roles as chiefs and council members. But—and this is a critical distinction—clan mothers appointed the chiefs and could depose them if they acted corruptly.

"The gantowisas (a word designating women in their official capacity) enjoyed sweeping political powers, which ranged from the administrative and legislative to the judicial," wrote Mann. They ran the local clan councils, nominated the chiefs to the men's council and could impeach wrongdoers. Mann invites readers to imagine what the US Congress would be like if contemporary women had the power retained by the Iroquois.

These and other female powers were established in the twelfth century when warring tribes came together to create the Iroquois (Haudenosaunee) League and agree to the Great Law of Peace, also known as the Constitution of the Five (later Six) Nations. This great event coincided with the adoption of agriculture, which profoundly shifted political and economic power toward women.[56]

"It was clear that women, alone, held veto powers over war," Mann wrote. They "controlled the peace by regulating the wars, appointing the warriors, declaring war and negotiating the peace that followed."[57] ...no war was ever called until after the women had unsuccessfully tried thrice to achieve a peaceful solution."

Most importantly, the men and women had parallel political structures that held separate councils and shared information through "speakers" who moved from one to the other.

In this and other ways, Iroquois men and women exercised equivalent power, balancing each other in sacred as well as secular spheres.

Such thoroughgoing equality was rooted in a principle that Mann called "Twinning," in which both genders were responsible for creating the universe. Twinning is so fundamentally different from the monotheism we know in Western life that it's hard to comprehend. The notion of one God, one spirit, one creator is supposed to be superior to two or more. The "one" is whole. Two are divided, while multiple "spirits" are seen as pagan in the Hebrew Christian tradition. But viewed from another perspective, two, or "twinning" suggests cooperation and cosmic balance.

Male and female bring their individual talents to the act of creation—a cooperative, not competitive, enterprise. The two principles balance each other, in the same way, that reality shifts between light and dark, smooth and complicated, easy and challenging, birthing and dying.

By comparison, one god compresses belief into a false pattern of unity that does not exist in nature. Western monotheism has always had this problem. It cannot explain pain except by externalizing it into "evil." God needs a devil to handle the bad stuff. And from the beginning, from Genesis in the Hebrew Bible, the male god needed to dominate both women and nature. It was and is a paradigm for patriarchy.

Mann is particularly negative about the generalized "Great Spirit" often attributed to modern Native beliefs, calling it a "minstrel version" of Iroquois concepts. By contrast with the oneness of Great Spirit, Iroquois stories involve four creators: Sky Woman, whose fall to earth creates Turtle Island (America), her daughter, Lynx, who generates the plants and flowers and her two grandsons, Sapling and Flint, who produce much of the rest of creation, working in tandem.

"Sapling tended to place only pleasant and convenient matters about the ground and in the waters. The gentle deer, flat trails, whispering breezes and smoother waters were his forte. Flint, on the other hand, tended to scatter rugged and difficult matters across Turtle's back, thrusting up high mountains, creating spectacular waterfalls and making the wind to blow in circles. It was only as each came after the other, alternating his brother's work, that their creations were perfected."[58]

The Iroquois concept of "twinning" doesn't rely on a rejected agent like the devil to explain the complexity of nature. Male and female figures in Iroquois creation stories work together, balancing each other, to bring the material world into being. There was no such thing as a devil in Iroquois belief systems, according to Mann. No concept of evil. In this sense, the Native belief system blends beautifully into modern ecological needs to retrieve a sense of sacredness in nature. Balance and cooperation make healthier partners than competition.

IN CHINA—THE MOSUO

As a rule, egalitarian cultures did not have marriage as we know it. In matrilineal societies where people traced linage through the mother's line, they often lived in clan houses headed by women. Lovers visited women at night and left in the light of dawn to return to their own clan houses. The children born from such unions were raised and fathered by uncles, so that all the parenting was carried out by brothers and sisters. Biological fathers may or may not have known which offspring came from their unions; nor did they have any authority over biological children; they were fathers to their own nieces and nephews.

To modern eyes, sexuality under these conditions looks like free love. Lovers came and went as they desired, romance appeared, then disappeared, as it is wont to do; women had full control of their bodies. There was no shame associated with sex.

"Women and men should not marry, for love is like the seasons—it comes and goes," wrote the authors of a marvelous memoir[59] about growing up in a modern matriarchal culture in southwest China, high up in the mountains at 10,000 feet, close to Tibet. The Moso, or Mosuo, are one of a few surviving examples of this very old mother-centered form of human culture. Children are raised by the mother's clan so they are never abandoned or put at risk by marital breakup.

Meanwhile, men and women can enjoy the pleasures of romantic, sexual union without obligation. There appear to be no examples of men abusing women, no rape, no physical attacks. When a woman did not want to see a particular lover again, she hung his bag outside her door and he did not come back.

"A Moso woman may have many lovers during her lifetime and she may have many children. Yet, each of them will perhaps have a different father and none of the fathers will live with his (biological) children," wrote Namu in her memoir.

> "Moso children should be raised in their mother's house and take the family name of their maternal ancestors. They should live side by side with their cousins—the children of their mother's sisters. The only men who live in the house are the brothers and uncles of the women. So in place of one father, Moso children have many uncles who take care of them."[60]

The first author of this memoir tells a compelling story of growing up in this mountain village. She tells of the love she bore her mother and of her equally urgent need to explore the wider world where she became a singer. With the help of Mathieu, an anthropologist, she makes clear that the matriarch in such cultures did not control anyone. She distributed the food and managed the house, but all decisions were made by the whole clan through consensus. The matriarch was chosen for each generation based on qualities of fairness and ability. "One should not think of my grandmother as a strict matriarch. In Moso families, decisions are always made in consultation with the other adults...Dabu (head females) do not really rule over anyone. Rather they are entrusted with responsibility because they are wise. My grandmother was Dabu, not because she was the oldest, and not only because she was a woman, but because among all her siblings, she was the smartest and the most capable."[61]

Men seemed to have liked this cultural system quite well, considering the resistance raised against attempts by the Communist Chinese government under Mao Zedong to import marriage and patriarchy into Moso life. Chinese cadres moved into the village and swamped the people with propaganda against free love, showing movies of syphilis, with faces being eaten away by infection. But as soon as Mao was dead, and the soldiers left, people happily went back to their old ways.

Mother-centered cultures run against the modern grain for a number of reasons, not just the lack of marriage or recognition of biological fatherhood. Many female academics looking at this kind of evidence go ballistic at the degree to which it locates female power in the home. They think it consigns women to a nurturing, generative role, too close to an earthly, biological nature—a philosophical stance they denigrate as "essentialism."

It's true that in these matriarchies, women usually did stay home, while men participated in long-distance trade and regional representation. That does not fit well with the need for women to assume positions of authority in our national and global life.

Like the author, Namu, we women of the modern age poured into the professional world in the past half-century, driven by the need to escape the confinement of home. In our society, matriarchal patterns like these cannot be duplicated because the home no longer holds economic resources. Nevertheless, there are important lessons to be learned.

One of the most significant implications is a mystery. If you believe, as I do, that individual men and women are not genetically programmed to be as different as we appear, then why have the two genders as a whole created such different cultures? Why have men created dominant, controlling societies while women produced egalitarian ones?

It's quite clear that women as a gender act democratically. The bugaboo of controlling mother power does not show up in societies organized around female authority. It's also worth noting that men in these cultures still have the responsibility for protecting their people. Women don't ordinarily have that task, and the key to what is responsible for the distinction between the kinds of societies created by men and women lies in this question: Who must fight and give his life for the good of the whole, and who must bear the next generation?

It's also clear that in cultures where women shared power with men there was a sacred female—a mirror in the spirit realm that reflected the authority wielded by women in everyday life. Among the Moso, it was a "mountain goddess," a geologic formation that rose over Lake Lugu near Namu's village. And each house was held up by sacred male and female columns that supported the roof—and by extension the sky.[62]

IN SUMATRA—THE MINANGKABAU

There is one very large ethnic group in the world that practices a form of matriarchy, which they have named a Matriarchaat, a Dutch word for the social organization of four million people in West Sumatra called the Minangkabau.

It looks nothing like patriarchy: women do not dominate the men. They exercise their leadership through elaborate ceremonies that emphasize and strengthen social networks among different clans. In this way, they also transmit the stories that guide the culture. Men have different leadership roles, meeting in all-male groups to implement the laws. And, in a particularly telling example, the men do not form hierarchies of power, even among themselves. They make decisions by consensus.

The Minangkabau is a matrilineal society—land ownership passes through the female line—so women have economic strength, an apparently critical foundation for female power. Older women have considerable authority in the clans, but brothers of mothers administer the land, as they do in many matrilineal societies of record. Children experience uncles as the ones with authority, while fathers love rather than teach. Uncles and fathers work the land together and men as a whole are often split between families of origin and families they marry into.

Although today the Minangkabau practice Islam, their origin myths depend on a legendary queen mother who is "the source of wisdom, the center of the universe," according to Peggy Reeves Sanday, who spent two decades visiting and studying this Indonesian ethnic group. The female founder had a foot in both earthly and spiritual realms, much like a divine king. But unlike Indo-European kings, her power "is not the power to subjugate but to conjugate—to knit together and to generate social ties in the here and now and in the hereafter. Seen in these terms, female power cannot be defined in terms of female dominance and male subordination. Rather, one finds interdependence and autonomy in both male and female domains, and maternal nurture constitutes the wellspring of social power," Sanday wrote in her ethnography.[63]

Several decades ago, Sanday had discovered an intimate relationship between female secular power and female divinity. Across 150 cultures the two came together, and the Minangkabau were no exception. While they spoke of an Islamic "God," they practiced the rituals that derived from belief in a mythical queen and her son. They seemed to have no trouble with this apparent paradox. In ceremonies many times a year, the women reenacted the legends that shaped their culture and embedded ethics of comity and goodwill. When force was needed—as in one story where rapacious thieves set upon the queen's companion—she called upon wild animals to help her defeat the enemy. Nature and the divine feminine were allies here, as in much of the ethnographic record where goddesses arose from the earth.

Administration of the law, done primarily by men in consultation with women, came about through a laborious process of reaching consensus. In one case, involving a bogus land claim, two men tried to take a piece of land by constructing a fake family tree. Their covert plan was to rent or sell the land, not allowed in Minangkabau traditions. It took villagers more than two years to reach a conclusion about the case, but when they did, they were able to enforce it by shunning an individual who would not cooperate. No jails, no police.

The culture, it seems, was unusually peaceable, with central values of respect and harmony. Sanday said that in her years of study she heard of only one instance of wife abuse. Rape was considered nonconsensual sex, the epitome of evil. To her knowledge, it did not occur. In the Indonesian environment, Islam supported these Minangkabau values.

COLONIALISM AND WOMEN'S RIGHTS

Women's power in egalitarian culture, including among the Iroquois, was systematically destroyed by European colonization. As patriarchy moved across the globe, European authorities chose to deal primarily with indigenous men, giving them the status westerners expected men to have. In the nineteenth century, for instance, the Maori of New Zealand registered their collective lands in the names of male tribal members to conform with British privatization laws. In one broad sweep, women lost any claim to their land.

"Prior to European settlement, Maori women could own land and had an equal voice in decision-making. However this was eroded with the arrival of European settlers and the imposition of a patriarchal western-based system which gave males/husbands the principal role in land transactions," writes Chandra K. Roy, a United Nations authority on indigenous women.[64]

A 2010 report on indigenous women[65] described how "with the gradual loss of collective ownership of lands and other natural resources and the introduction by dominant outsiders of institutions of private property, indigenous women progressively lost their traditional rights to lands and natural resources. The following has been a familiar pattern in many indigenous communities:

As the indigenous economy...weakened, male members of some indigenous communities became sole inheritors of lands and other property. As a result, female members have been deprived of their rights of traditional access to lands and other resources."

It hurts to write this, to realize that along with the agonizing casualties visited upon native peoples came additional losses of sexual equality and decent treatment of women for all of us. These are not just things that benefit women. They help men too in setting a more level playing field among them. In systems of gender equality, men do not separate into hierarchies of power and influence; equality is broad-based, affecting both sexes.

EQUALITY

In the female-empowered societies of the modern era that I refer to here, people made decisions by consensus of the whole, a fundamentally different process from that of a male-dominated chiefdom. In many societies, both ancient and modern, men and women held equivalent, but not the same, roles.

Men were/are often the ones who represented their clans to outside groups, or who traveled long distances for trade, built the houses, tended the animals and hunted. A designation as "chief" did not suggest unusual power. Rather the authority of a chief, usually male, came from mother-headed clans where decisions were made by consensus and carried out by men. This appears to be a form of direct democracy, according to many descriptions of indigenous groups that traced linage through the female line and placed the distribution of goods and food in the hands of a matriarch.

Such descriptions have been brought together and analyzed in a single volume by German philosopher and religious historian Heide Göettner-Abendroth.[66] Translated into English only recently, this huge body of work finally compiles into one source all the known characteristics of extant "mother-centered" cultures in Asia, Africa, the Pacific and the Americas. Europe and the Near East lost such cultures so long ago that none survived into the recent historical past, meaning since the nineteenth century, when records began to be kept.

FLUID GENDER DISTINCTIONS

Despite their importance in revealing the existence and character of female-empowered culture, the structure of these societies may strike an odd note in today's world. Clans no longer exist—whether derived from male or female linage. We have trouble building communities where people know each other enough to say hello. Marriage and fatherhood are deeply embedded, not likely to be transformed into a matrilineal style.

Nevertheless, there are critical lessons to be learned from these female-centered societies. They teach us what men and women can be like in a state of equality, when males are not taught to disrespect and dominate the female.

Genes do not structure gender behavior. This is evident not only from the immense variety seen in ethnographic societies, but in any cursory review of the genetics of behavior. Genes for all personality traits are malleable, responsive to the impact of regulator genes that operate in the environment, open to cultural influences after birth. Gender behavior is no different. If men can be induced by culture to sacrifice their most basic instinct for the welfare of their group, then what trait could possibly be genetically driven? What is more basic than the will to life itself?

But if nature hasn't given us our gender traits, culture certainly has. We are different kinds of people in a patriarchy, struggling all the time to escape from the restraints imposed by gender roles. What the lived experience of people in equal societies seems to be telling us is that women have never ruled over men and don't aspire to such power. We do want to share the power with men in creating a wholly different culture of equality.

Chief among the qualities of an equal culture is the *lack of gender distinctions*. Patriarchy erects radical cultural distinctions between men and women that do not stem from biology. Equality takes men and women in the opposite direction, toward a fluid state where gender roles very nearly disappear, except for those directly related to childbearing.

We men and women are not very different except for the marvelous sexual distinctions and attractions that drive the creation of life. That is what the evidence of cultural equality seems to say. Without armies or tribal feuds, men are as peaceable and tuned to the natural world as women are. Both have a dark side; both can be aggressive. What makes men different is cultural training for war. What stands out as the force driving male dominance is militarism.

So, let me rephrase a central question. Rather than asking what the world would be like if women ran it, let's ask: What would men be like if they did not have to be trained for war?

ELEVEN

OF MEN AND MASCULINITY

One morning recently, I was sitting quietly in meditation as I normally do, focusing on my breath moving in and out, when, suddenly I couldn't breathe! Fear flashed through my mind followed by the thought, "If I can't breathe, I will die!" I leaped from my chair gasping and struggling for air. Finally my lungs expanded and I took the air in gratefully, along with an overwhelming rush of sadness and grief. The feelings were close and personal; they were about losing God!

I was stunned. How could this be? I am eighty years old. I've been a feminist for nearly half a century. I don't appreciate patriarchal belief systems, whether secular or divine. I left God when I was seventeen, walking out on a white-bearded evangelical minister who was waving his arms at the front of the Presbyterian Church in Pasadena, California, calling people to atone for their sins. I was disgusted and I never returned to that sort of religion. So why was I mourning this male God of Christianity?

In subsequent days, I began to put together the connections my subconscious had been hiding over these many years. My brain had connected marriage, husband and God into one male dominant package—all of which I had rejected as a young woman. Though I'd had several monogamous unions in my life, I never married, never followed the patterns set out for a woman coming of age in the 1950s. Instead I pursued a career in journalism and anthropology, always keeping alive the hope that I would find a man with whom I could achieve equality. For me the idea of "wife" was tainted with a threat of losing independence.

Four days before the breathing incident, I had taken a therapeutic trip with psychedelic mushrooms, intending to put this lifelong search for the Right Man to rest. I knew with some part of my mind that it was an adolescent search and I needed help in making the subconscious connections.

The trip had been horrible! I saw myself dead, buried under the ground with my arm reaching out of the dirt for help. My guide—an attractive young woman—appeared to me with scant white hair falling off her head. I didn't know what this experience meant other than the obvious message that I didn't have much time left. Better not waste it!

But now, days later, I had come to an astounding new meaning. In fact, I had to grieve the death of God if I were to let go of the old idea that the right man could "save" me, could provide the wisdom and guidance I needed. Husband and God were joined in a way I had never understood—until I opened this deep-seated mental lock with a psychedelic medicine.

I didn't come easily to a pioneering stance for a woman of my era. As detailed in chapter two, my life had been traumatized by the death of my younger sister when I was thirteen and by the subsequent dysfunction of my parents and family. I struggled through a deep sense of abandonment, taking refuge in learning and intellect. The last thing I wanted as a young woman was to marry and have children. I wanted to experience the world! I wanted an identity, nothing like the role of "wife"—a person who in my mind had no name.

I saw so many college-educated women of my generation choose marriage and motherhood and then move out into the new post-war suburbs, where they fell into loneliness and alcoholism, dependent on husbands who ran the world outside. I wanted none of it. If I had married, I knew I was supposed to give away my power to a partner. Especially if I married an upwardly mobile man (as I was supposed to do), I would have felt compelled to follow him, to extoll his creativity, his intelligence, his agency, while diminishing my own. That's what I thought we women should do, and the men in my generation expected it too. To make matters more difficult psychologically, I was born of a mother who dominated my father and I never stopped trying to make him stand tall in my mind.

Before I left in my twenties for a career on the East Coast, I visited my father in his workplace to ask for his blessing and wisdom. He said to me, "I'm afraid I can't help you. I've been a failure in my life." I was devastated. Even now his comment hurts my soul. He died in 1972, gone before I filled the vessel in my heart named "father." I don't know how I would have done that; I only know I didn't try after that early visit. I mourn that loss.

But if equality with a man was not available to me, sexual connection was always available in a series of monogamous unions that each lasted years, sometimes in common residence, more often not. As time passed, men with equivalent education and social status were less and less available, even if I could have retained a sense of personal power and agency with them. More than once, I fell into a love affair with a man who drank too much. The truth is that I used my head in my professional life, but not so much in the romantic realm.

I don't like being single. Although I have a rich community life, with truly wonderful neighbors and lots of activities, the deep places where intimacy connects us with loving contentment are unfilled, temporarily. I say "temporarily" because twice in the past ten years I have had such a partner that filled my deep need for connection. The first one succumbed to alcoholism and the last one, Paul, died at the end of 2019. I am alone again, looking for love, looking for equality with a man. I will probably *die* this way, I say to myself on my bad days.

To be fair, though, I have learned how to love in a way that transcends the individual; to see my partner as part of a universe of love, both single and many. Paul believed that, and was a truly beautiful soul, intelligent, accomplished, and as warm-hearted as they come. A doctor of rehabilitative medicine, he had given his life generously in the service of handicapped people. He'd been taught how to be a feminist by his deceased wife and let me know that I didn't have to take care of him. And, in many ways for the first time, I let him take care of me. Freedom, companionship, love and equality—we had it all. He is with me still in spirit, as is my former loving partner, Philip, who died more recently, in July of 2020.

On the road named "True Love," I have moved from hating my femininity to tenderly reapproaching and redefining the concept. Once it meant weakness, which drove many of us women to run from the idea. Since those days, I have come to define "feminine" as whoever and whatever I am. I own the concept. I can interpret it any way I wish. I love men; therefore I am feminine. I am powerful, therefore I am feminine. I feel emotionally connected to others, therefore I am feminine. I want physical touching and sex; therefore I am feminine.

I pray for boys growing up now to have the same freedom. They don't all have it yet, as Peggy Orenstein's study of adolescent boyhood demonstrates.[67] Boys she studied in upper middle class schools are currently being conditioned by each other to display "toxic masculinity," which means among other things to disrespect the "feminine" and abuse women sexually. Even if fathers or other adult men no longer abused them, as they did in the Iatmul culture and in our own past, it's still the case that these boys are getting abused—now by peers.

The culture acts through adolescent behavior to traumatize youth, to scare them away from acting like "pussies" by turning sexuality into a sporting game in which they pound and attack—i.e., beat up and control women's sexual natures. It is brutal. It is the source of an assault on nature and women. It is the fertilizer that feeds patriarchy.

Sexuality in its most fundamental aspects is the source of all life. When young men learn "manhood" by disrespecting feminine attributes so ferociously, we are lead ultimately to war, competition, hierarchy and abuse of the earth. I have no doubt that young boys need to display and develop strength. But that can be done without teaching them that "pussy" is equivalent to weak. Iroquois boys learned to be strong, to be hunters, to withstand pain—all without learning to disrespect women. It was remarkable at the time how Iroquois children were treated by parents—as little people with their own rights. They had freedom to be themselves, rather than being a controlled version of an adult, moderated by their elders.

The deep sadness of male life in a patriarchal system is that while it seems to give men extra power over women, only a few benefit. The hierarchy of authority brings as much grief for the vast majority of men down the totem pole as it does for women who are considered second class. In fact, men are its first victims. Those on the losing side periodically revolt in efforts to readjust the inequality; unfortunately, it can't be readjusted through violence.

Since the 1980s, a growing wealth gap has been evident, leading to ever greater economic stratification. Harvard Business School professor Rosabeth Moss Kantor described the approaching disparity some twenty years ago, when she divided the population into "cosmopolitans" who knew how to work in the global economy and "locals" who did not.[68]

Observing this process in the past two decades has been like watching a slow-moving train wreck. Today, so many of these men still see themselves "standing in line," as sociologist Arlie Russell Hochschild described it in her ethnography of men in Louisiana.[69] They are waiting for the rewards they have been promised in a male-dominated world, still believing that private enterprise will come through for them, even while corporations pollute their lands and sicken their children. Meanwhile, they hate government, concluding that social policies have shoved them down, allowing women and minorities to cut into line ahead of them. It's hard to see how this process ends well, considering that we are mentally surrounded on a daily basis by threat, division and propaganda.

We can hope that equality for women might drive in the other direction, toward greater stability and increased equality for all. What else have we got? The good news is that it is happening anyway. We need to balance each other. As empowered individuals, men and women together can hold up the sky with greater equilibrium.

WE CAN'T DO IT ALONE

In this time of ecological threat, with dire predictions of significant climate disruption within our lifetimes, we need to retrieve the sanctity of the earth. And to do that, women need the help of men. We can't do it alone. More than once recently, I've heard men defer to women, hoping that female leadership will lead us out of this quagmire and into a safer future. I've no doubt that will help, but female leadership alone will not solve the problem. Male culture has to change. Without the help of men, the forces of patriarchy are overwhelming. Women who challenge these forces either begin to conform or get thrown out. After each feminist historical period, patriarchy returns to write and rewrite women out of the action, again and again. Hierarchy, the handmaid of patriarchy, benefits elites who control the resources. While wealth dominates culture, we do not have a chance of saving ourselves or the Earth.

One important aspect of Iroquois training of children was their emphasis on individuality. Nothing is more important to our survival now than training boys to be individuals, as girls have learned over the past fifty years.

My mind spins with the painful stories currently told of growing up masculine, living with the violence, and yet privilege, of being born an American white man. Now, in the fourth year of the Trump presidency, we gag on public displays of hatred for other races and the threat of terrorism from home-grown Americans. The worst qualities of male-dominant culture are in our faces every day. At least, we can finally see the problem at the heart of masculinity in a powerful way, as told by individuals struggling with having to grow past the stereotypes.

Hard notions of masculinity must be redefined by every individual as he moves through his life. Any idea of "learning to be a man" is dangerous, based as it is on command and destroy qualities, dictated by a hierarchy of cultural elites. Rigid cultural prescriptions for masculinity will continue the process of destruction, of women as well as the Earth. There is no such thing as one way of being masculine. You can't reshape the idea; you can only leave it to the individual.

I haven't found the process of divorcing from cultural sex roles to be easy. It seems to impinge upon one's sense of sexuality, especially when young. I remember becoming agitated about the loss when I was in graduate school studying hominid evolution. I ran into my professor's office one day, asking him what we would do as men and women if we lost our sex roles. He said not to worry, sexual attraction remains, even if the roles disappear. We don't have to be one way or the other, as masculine or feminine people. We can be ourselves and the system still works. Mother Nature has bred the differences into us—the energy that draws us together, no matter what the cultural roles may be.

COPING WITH MODERN PATRIARCHY

I don't mean to say that redefining the way boys learn masculinity will solve all the problems we have with hierarchy and global threat in massive modern states. That will help, but so much more is needed in terms of good political practices, which are beyond the scope of this book. However, to create better democratic processes in this country, I believe we have to reduce the level of social, public aggression that we tolerate on the part of men. Too often we accept—and even endorse—male expressions of anger and violence.

You may say that we need such aggression in order to survive a threat from the outside. But actually the threat is from the inside—from the classic "protector" role for men that moves us ever closer to global annihilation. Just as women have to control reproduction to reduce the outsized human population on Earth, so do white men have to change their historic recourse to physical/emotional aggression as a way of preserving their cultural dominance.

It's asking a lot, I know. But we can help ourselves by telling different stories about who we are as human beings. That's my purpose here—to ferret out and bring together the stories of cooperation that writers and academics have created about our human past—the ones that keep getting written out of the canon.

Nowhere has this tendency to write female empowerment out of the record been more pronounced in recent years than in the story of the Neolithic goddess. This nature deity, revived through scholarship since the 1970s, has inspired women and men far beyond academic circles and remains an important way to readjust the balance with all-male gods. Loss of such evidence damages our human record.

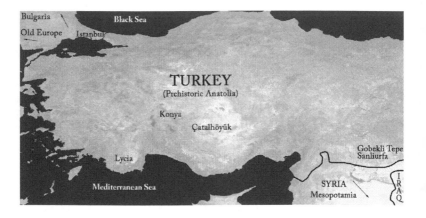

TWELVE

THE BACKLASH

I am in despair. I went back into the Neolithic to retrieve my knowledge of the goddess that so inspired me 40 years ago only to find that her existence had been totally deconstructed in the meantime by authorities in the field. Not only that, but I am faced with a trove of penises from a very ancient site that puts a phallic twist on this previously female-centered era. The year was mid-2017 and President Trump was well on his way to dismantling all the environmental protections designed to save the Earth. In the sacred, as well as the secular realm, women were screwed.

While I, among many, luxuriated in the administration of Barack Obama, a patriarchal backlash was building in the country. It so happened—as it often does—that a similar backlash was sweeping the academic world, rewriting the anthropology of female power.

Cultural history is maintained for us in university studies and records over hundreds of years. In Western society, men have been the primary and sometimes the only actors in that history. So it is not difficult for determined champions of patriarchy to write women out of the history books, if they happen to sneak in from time to time. This has certainly been true for the historic period, as Gerda Lerner showed in her extraordinary book, *The Creation of Feminist Consciousness.*[70]

As I researched material for this memoir, I found that a similar process had been going on for the prehistoric period before the creation of patriarchy, led by academic anthropologists and archaeologists who have contradicted the evidence, provided principally by Marija Gimbutas and James Mellaart, of goddess worship during the Neolithic in Europe and the Middle

East. Working site by site, year after year, members of prominent departments in universities like Stanford, the University of California and others began to take the goddess story apart. It has been a nasty process, including ridicule and obfuscation, which gained speed in the decades since Gimbutas's death in 1994.

Religious philosopher Charlene Spretnak wrote of hearing archaeologists at a conference on gender in 2002 "whoop with laughter" during a sarcastic presentation that demeaned Gimbutas's work. In 2011,[71] Spretnak detailed the backlash, writing that after Gimbutas's death, "she was relentlessly misrepresented in the extreme, pilloried for holding positions that she repeatedly argued against, and demeaned and dismissed—beginning first with a small group of professors and spreading to such an extent that her work is no longer read, assigned, or cited in the classes of many Anglo-American professors of European archaeology." The idea of a Neolithic goddess has been termed "outdated," "sexist," even "dotty."

This change appears intentional, a deliberate effort to reinterpret every artifact identified as a "goddess." Some artifacts are no longer "female" but identified as "animals"; others have "ambiguous" gender traits; still others can be seen as male or simply adult women.

It's as if they have taken a fire hose to the goddess.

Those who know or have written about the prehistoric sacred female have watched the takedown of this grand theory with alarm. Religious scholar Anne Barstow wrote to me,

"I am appalled at how narrow-minded the archaeologists are today: tone-deaf to religion and downright hostile to any evidence of female power. They almost sound afraid of it. It's over simple to say this is misogyny; yet what else can one conclude?"

In her work, Gimbutas had gathered together those "old, old gods" and offered them to us as the Goddess/Creatrix of prehistory. This deity was both multiple and singular: the bird and snake goddesses—the Great Mother goddess. Gimbutas said they were symbols, *not* women. This is a nature religion, she wrote. It is based on the female. There is no evidence whatsoever for a father God. Her books and ideas burst through the walls of academe in the

'80s and '90s, giving support to a burgeoning feminist movement that craved such rich descriptions of female divinity.

Gimbutas's theories, however, went far beyond artifacts. She described a prehistoric civilization where women were honored, not dominated, in cultures of peace and stability—a golden age, so to speak, when women and nature were central in the lives of Europeans. This world came crashing down when male-dominated groups from the Russian steppes north of the Black Sea (now Ukraine) invaded Eastern Europe, bringing fundamental changes in language, culture and religion. This Kurgan invasion (Gimbutas took the name from their burial mounds, called kurgans) led to the establishment of Indo-European languages and patriarchy during the Bronze Age. These changes took place over 2,000 years in more than one incursion, according to Joan Marler, Gimbutas's editor and founder/director of the Institute of Archaeomythology in northern California.[72]

"The stable, egalitarian, matricentric cultures of Neolithic Europe were replaced by patriarchal patterns of dominance although Old European patterns continued as substratum elements in subsequent European societies," Marler wrote.

The silence that followed Gimbutas's goddess publications lasted about ten years. Then the reactive flood began. For the past twenty years, the Lithuanian archaeologist has been pounded with negative attention from her colleagues in the field, who have leapfrogged over each other in their eagerness to prove the goddess theories wrong.

THE MYSTERIES OF PREHISTORY

Without writing, the truth cannot be validated with objective evidence. Unlike academics in a scientific field like physics, archaeologists working at prehistoric sites have no means of proving their theories with precise empirical data. The objects they study come to us without written script and are mostly mute. Experts "read" them dimly through their own projections, attempting as best they can to relate them to the context of the site in which they are found. For the most part, the stratigraphy or geological layers at the site do not tell much about the function of these artifacts.

The result is a wildly various view of the past. The thousands of objects Gimbutas drew upon in writing her books about the Great Goddess have been described as everything from dolls to idols. Examples of reinterpretation are legion. One involves a circle of figures—all female—from around 6,500 years ago, (c. 4,900-4,200 BCE) in the area that is now Romania. They all look alike or very similar. Long thin bodies on top, very large hips, slight facial features, no arms, bodies covered with spirals, the figures lean back in chairs arranged in a circle, as though they are in council. In fact, they have been called the "The Council of Goddesses," by European archaeologists, as well as by Gimbutas.

One critic, American archaeologist Douglass Bailey, contended in a 2010 analysis that the figures do not represent a cult or deity, but were used to "create a shared understanding of group identity.... They stated without words, but in always present visual and tactile expression, 'This is us.'"[73]

Bailey continued, "While these figurines were powerful objects, that power rested not in any specific reference to the divine, but rather in their condition as miniature objects... facilitating deep-seated understandings of what is appropriate in terms of body appearance and membership within a group."

More recently,[74] Bailey retracted his earlier theory, admitting that his interpretations of the figurines as defining group identity is no more valid than Gimbutas's interpretation of cult figures in a female-centered spiritual world.

Finally, Bailey just gave up completely on trying to find meaning and resorted to using the figurines in artistic play, combining the ancient with contemporary objects. At one point, he paired the Neolithic figurines with Barbie dolls and attempted to show them in an exhibit. His efforts were thwarted, however, when museum authorities would not allow such a display.

To give the critics their due, interpreting and reinterpreting objects like this is their business. One can't expand the field without new ways of seeing artifacts. But they face a physical trove of thousands of objects from thousands of years in the past, the vast majority of which indicate female form. There are few representations of males, though many that combine animal with female features. So many artifacts from across a broad swath of ancient Europe and the Near East have similarities in form and appearance that it is logical to conclude they represented religious concepts centered on the creation of life. Moreover, the figures often carry a phallic sign in the shape of a cylindrical head, on top of a female body.

That has not stopped academics from discrediting such a belief system—never more clear than in a recent edition of the esteemed *Oxford Handbook on Prehistoric Figurines*, published in 2017. In the handbook's introductory article, Richard Lesure of UCLA (where Gimbutas did her own work) generates a stunning metaphor for the goddess that aptly illustrates the level of disrespect with which this story is now held.

Arguing that archaeologists haven't been able to "kill" (his word) the goddess with their site-by-site analyses, Lesure recommends that they find a new "grand history" of human evolution that could match it. With cheery academic malevolence, he compares the assault on the "Goddess thesis" with the murder of Grigori Rasputin, a "creepy Russian mystic whose actions were rocking the already tottering Romanov dynasty in the early twentieth century." Rasputin apparently survived multiple efforts to kill him, including stab wounds and poisoning. He finally succumbed to bullets.

"Likewise with the Goddess," Lesure writes, "the perception among analysts is that she lives on despite one mortal wound after another…the Goddess staggers on (because) among Neolithic figurines of the ancient Near East and beyond there is systematic patterning at a very large scale—at the scale indeed at which the goddess construct was formulated.

"Interpreters who perpetuate the Goddess construct do so because they sense those larger coherences. We should thus stop stabbing the goddess with the dagger of context. *That is never going to kill her off* (my ital.). She will only fade away for good when we devise an alternative grand history that accounts for large scale coherences."[75]

Along the way, Lesure noted that these shared "coherences" do not represent divinity but perhaps were tied to magic. Oh really? One person's magic is another person's God or Goddess. Using terms like "magic" or "cult" is the archaeologists' way of distancing themselves from any hint of "religion."

Finding a new grand theory, however, will not be easy, simply because the objects cannot say who and what they are. Modern humans have to create the stories, and some narratives are better than others. In the end, one has to admit clear and abundant evidence of female divinity, as do the editors of the book, *Ancient Goddesses: The Myths and the Evidence*, (University of Wisconsin Press, 1999), a volume of archaeological professionals who critically analyze Gimbutas's work, including several opponents from major California universities. The editors write, "most of the contributors found strong evidence for female divinities,"[76] using the plural to indicate diversity.

In 2017, the tide began to turn a bit for Gimbutas and her work. New DNA evidence from ancient European skeletons confirmed her thesis that people from the Russian steppes invaded Eastern Europe in the prehistoric era.[77] This was a conquest by men (sex ratio, 10-1), called the Yamnaya, who very rapidly spread their genes into established European populations[78] as far as Germany. They came in 3,000 to 1,000 BCE, riding newly domesticated horses and over time transformed the earlier cultures, spreading Indo-European language and laying the foundation for classical civilization.[79] Their DNA is widespread in Europeans today. In early Russia, as elsewhere in the world, steppe people were pastoralists, a type of livelihood associated with male dominance.

With the invasion hypothesis proven to be genetically valid, the gate was opened to reconsideration of Gimbutas's other claims. In an important 2017 lecture at Chicago's Oriental Institute, Lord Colin Renfrew from Cambridge University, an early critic of Gimbutas and a leader in archaeology, used words that lit up the field of feminist spirituality. He said she showed "remarkable insight" in describing the Kurgan invasion and that her work on the origins of Indo-European language had been "magnificently vindicated."[80]

Hopefully, this will give "permission to other scholars to reconsider all of Gimbutas's theories and perhaps eventually to restore her to her rightful place as one of the most —if not *the* most—creative, scientific, groundbreaking archaeologists of the twentieth century," wrote religious scholar Carol Christ, a defender of Gimbutas, in an article titled "Marija Gimbutas Triumphant: Colin Renfrew Concedes."[81]

DECONSTRUCTING THE GODDESS AT ÇATALHÖYÜK

Gimbutas's work is not the only goddess narrative that has been deconstructed. There's also Mellaart's work at Çatalhöyük, where apparently a prehistoric goddess thrived in an egalitarian culture of considerable size. But, in the past twenty years of excavation, the Stanford team headed by Hodder has reinterpreted the material remains at Çatalhöyük. In the process, they have written the goddess out of it.

How can they do that? You may wonder, who's right? Well, it's a matter of how you see things. The rooms that Mellaart called "shrines" were not shrines, according to Hodder. They are rooms, just like any other room in houses that are all decorated pretty much alike, with the same figures, same wall decorations. By implication, the sacred cannot be separated from the mundane. You don't know what things were worshipped.

To make it really difficult, the people of Çatalhöyük left us with a mystery that reverberates down through the centuries to our own time. They removed the faces, hands and feet of the bas-relief wall figures that Mellaart called goddesses. Each time these ancient people plastered over and refurbished their walls, the defining characteristics of the wall figures were lost. Thus, we are left with an ambiguous figure that has a human outline, but is it human? Is it female?

"It is a bear," said Hodder. What? A bear? Not a goddess? I can't stand this. This is when I decided to go to Stanford to interview Hodder. What follows are more quotes from our conversation in his office.

The goddess/bear tantalizes the viewer with its arms and legs splayed out in a horizontal fashion as if the figure is jumping for joy. There are many of them in different houses at Çatalhöyük; in one of them the figure's navel is encircled with a spiral as though indicating a womb.

I asked if the spiral indicated pregnancy or womb.

"Maybe," said Hodder.

The arms are held up in a classical position of worship. The legs appear to be giving birth.

"What does that mean to you?" I asked.

"Nothing in particular," he replied. "It's difficult to know what interpretation was made by the people then. The only evidence we have of what those things actually represented is the stamp seal."

Oh, I see. This is the basis for a "bear" interpretation. Excavators found a stamp seal in the debris on the floor that shows a bear figure in the exact same position with arms and legs raised. Unlike the mysterious figures on the wall, the stamp seal has claws and a head depicting a bear.

"Could the wall relief be a hybrid, a female bear?" I asked.

"Yes."

"Is it likely?"

"We have no evidence that it is either female or male."

"But there's a circle around the naval," I protested.

Unwilling to commit himself, Hodder said, "Only one figure has a circle around the naval. Most of them don't."

Apparently, one is not enough here, nor in the case of the most famous goddess figure of all from Çatalhöyük, the seated figure with arms resting on lion heads with a skull between the feet. There is only one like that. And there's only one of a third figure, the upper body of a female with a skeleton carved into its back.

"It's very intriguing—the idea that women had some special relationship with the dead…but at Çatalhöyük, we don't have that evidence, so it's difficult to make the case. I wish we could say more about that."

Hodder did, however, have a great deal to say about phalluses at Çatalhöyük, which are painted onto wild animals in wall scenes depicting hunts. All the phalluses are on animal figures on wall paintings, not on any human images. Nevertheless, Hodder said, "If you look at these figures, there are just as many phalluses as there are other sorts of figurines."

At the end of the interview, I was stunned to hear Hodder's interpretation of a figurine unearthed in 2016 from a grave at Çatalhöyük. Described as a "Goddess" in news reports, the fat stone figure has arms crossed under big breasts, but no triangle in the vagina region. No penis either.

"Most people would see this as a female, but there's no evidence it's female," said Hodder. "There's no vagina, actually no sexual characteristics. The breasts could be interpreted as male breasts…It looks like a Sumo wrestler." I looked at him in shock.

At home, I googled pictures of Sumo wrestlers. Hodder was right; they have awfully big breasts. But it's hard to imagine that men in the Neolithic would become so fat. And seen from the back, the big hips and buttocks of the figurine look decidedly female. No Sumo wrestler has hips like that.

Hundreds of the figurines at Çatalhöyük have been

reinterpreted by Hodder's team over the past twenty years, dramatically reducing the number identified as female. The Neolithic—an era once identified with the prehistoric goddess—has come to be seen by Hodder as a phallocentric period. Not all archaeologists agree with Hodder that the Neolithic was phallocentric, but in devaluing the work of Gimbutas and Mellaart, they have effectively eliminated any interpretation of goddess worship during the Agricultural Revolution.

Nor is that the end of the gender reversal of the past two decades. To make matters even more challenging for goddess theorists, a massive archaeological site was uncovered in 1994 in the Near East, which puts a male-dominated image directly on the Neolithic center stage. It has been called the world's first "temple" by *Smithsonian Magazine* and others. Constructed at an unimaginably early time, 11,500 years ago (9,500 BCE), the site dates to just before the rise of agriculture and human settlement. There's no evidence that anyone lived there, but they may well have worshipped at this place, called Göbekli Tepe.

A STONE AGE TEMPLE

Located in the desert near the borders of Turkey and Syria, Göbekli Tepe is like a giant Rorschach test for the human race. Among the interpretations generated: an observatory for ancient peoples to view the heavens; a memorial to a comet impact on the Earth; a vision anticipating the Garden of Eden; a sign of the coming of the Gods and human mastery over nature. The list goes on, but what stands out over and over again is gender. Göbekli Tepe seems to be male, all male. There is no sign of the Neolithic goddess. Therefore, she did not exist.

I will come back to this phallocentric view of Göbekli Tepe in a moment, but first let me describe this astounding installation, the very first construction in human history. There's little doubt that Göbekli Tepe is a sanctuary. Our first evidence of prehistoric people moving toward civilization is not homes, not markets, not walls—but religion. The place is huge. More than sixty monumental pillars up to thirteen feet high, each weighing many tons, have so far been uncovered. Many more remain buried on the site, as many as 200. The monuments stand upright in the dirt, covered with carvings of animals such as lions, boars, scorpions, snakes, lizards and foxes, some with their mouths and teeth in a snarl, some with erect penises. It is the animal penises that convey a strongly masculine character since the handful of human figures found at Göbekli Tepe have no genitals.

Above and around all of these animal figures (including several human heads), is the abstract representation of a human being, with arms down the sides of the pillars and a belt across the middle. Experts identify the pillars as abstract anthropomorphic images, with low relief carvings of arms, hands, and items of clothing, such as belts and loincloths. The top stone crosspiece on two of these monolithic figures, standing fifteen feet tall, seems to represent a human head.

A blog maintained by the excavation research staff, called *The Tepe Telegrams*, gives this description:[82] "The oblong T-heads can be regarded as abstract depictions of the human head, the smaller side representing the face. Clearly visible are arms on the pillars' shafts with hands brought together above the abdomen. The depiction of belts and loincloths in the shape of animal skins underlines the impression that these T-shaped pillars own an anthropomorphic identity."

The monuments look like spiritual beings—male spiritual beings. The *Telegram* article continues: "Thus, it is highly probable to assume that the pair of pillars in Enclosure D should represent two male individuals. Indeed, it seems striking that the iconographic and symbolic world present at Göbekli Tepe is one dominated by masculinity. Whenever the gender of one of the animals depicted is indicated, it is a male specimen."

Where did these things come from? Who did them? What do they mean?

The "who" were ancient hunters and gatherers who had not even built towns yet and were only beginning the process of domesticating plants and animals. It was not believed they had the skills or organizational power to lug huge pillars of stone, weighing many tons, from the nearby mountains and set them up in circles on the open plain. But there it is. The meaning is much more difficult to decipher—one might say impossible. It certainly seems to be devotional, but who or what was worshipped?

My first impulse was to see these giant figures as supernatural, though I have no belief in such things. Still, the feeling comes up, and I remember the image in the movie, *2001: A Space Odyssey*, where babbling proto-humans confront a mysterious megalith. In wondrous confusion, they circle the black monolith that suddenly rises from the empty plain, not unlike us moderns who look upon Göbekli Tepe and search for ways to explain it.

One observer,[83] an engineer from Scotland, has suggested that it's an observatory. The figures are zodiac symbols, he says, representing the night sky and constellations. He has done a lot of computer matching and says that one of the monoliths (which includes a scorpion) compares with the stars as they would have appeared in the year 10,950 BC. But then, someone else pointed out that all the monoliths were unstable and had moved slightly so computer matching wouldn't really work. Moreover, the circles into which the monoliths have been placed are irregular, unlike the perfect circles that would have been created by even these early people in order to observe the heavens.

But, of course, the story belongs to the one who does the excavating and that man, the late Klaus Schmidt of the German Archaeological Institute, focused on animal penises. The figures with erect penises were not animals that people would normally have hunted for food, but more dangerous predators such as boars, leopards and foxes. The scorpions, lizards, snakes ducks and birds carved into the columns were not sexed. Though the giant human depictions lack penises, they appear to be male, judging by the belt across the middle. Off in the corner, on a low flat stone, is a strange drawing of a woman. Her figure is scratched onto the stone rather than carved. She is a lone female and a rather sad one at that, an awkward figure situated on a low stone bench.

"We don't have female symbolism at Göbekli," said Schmidt in a lecture at an international symposium on the site in 2012. "It doesn't mean females were not important here during the Neolithic, but they're not seen on these sculptures."[84]

The Great Goddess remains invisible.

To make matters more difficult for those of us in search of the divine female, Göbekli Tepe lies a short drive from the place, formerly called Ur, where Abraham was born, beginning the age of patriarchal religion, and where Enheduanna worshipped Inanna more than 6,000 years after the huge monoliths were built.

Publicly, Schmidt refrained from making religious interpretations, but others who went to Göbekli Tepe and talked to him came back more than once with some version of the Garden of Eden. Skirting a biblical interpretation, Schmidt pointed out that the huge, otherworldly human bodies carved onto two of the monoliths seem to tower over all the other animals. During earlier art in the Paleolithic, "animals are dominant; now the human is the boss...humans are the superior form."

In a *National Geographic* documentary called "Göbekli Tepe, Angels N Demons" archaeologist Jeffrey Rose concluded his story of the site with this astounding statement: "Instead of being just part of the natural world, we are beginning to see ourselves as masters of it ....under these towering pillars, we gave birth to the Gods."[85] *National Geographic* has thus given us a new story of heretofore uncounted centuries of Biblical religion. It isn't enough that we've had to tolerate 3,500 years of patriarchy in the spiritual realm. Here's another 8,000 years to contemplate. Thank you very much.

I went into the Neolithic to find the sacred female and her relationship with the natural world. Instead I found the gods of

Abraham. Busloads of evangelical Christian tourists go to the site because they view Göbekli Tepe as material proof of the Garden of Eden. Fortunately, some archaeologists, like Brian Rose of the University of Pennsylvania, want to halt the biblical interpretations. "There's no connection between the Garden of Eden and Göbekli Tepe," Rose said. "This is not Genesis."[86]

Okay, but we are still left with what appears to be male dominance.

Hodder also went to Göbekli Tepe, bringing back the story of phalluses, along with new interpretations of hunting scenes on the walls at Çatalhöyük that focus on the erect penises of the hunted animals. He also found that the same jumping bear figure found at Çatalhöyük 400 miles away was carved onto a pillar of stone at Göbekli Tepe. It had been created some 2,000 years before Çatalhöyük even existed. Emphasizing the phallic nature of Göbekli, Schmidt had shown him a pit full of phalluses dug out of the dirt. Maybe they had not been attached yet. Who knows?

It's a phallocentric era, Hodder wrote in 2011, in a jointly authored article with Lynn Meskill, also a Stanford archaeologist. "We suggest that current data do not support the traditional ideas of fertility and matriarchy that have long been associated with discussions of the emergence of settled agricultural life. Rather, current data present a picture of animality and phallic masculinity that downplays female centrality...we refer to the privileging of maleness as a prime cultural signifier and the centrality of masculinity (both human and animal) as a source of power and authority within the material and symbolic repertoire of the Turkish Neolithic."

This is bad, but it gets worse.

Hodder and Meskill go on to describe the one little female figure scratched onto a stone at Göbekli Tepe:

"The only clearly female image at Göbekli was incised on a stone slab on a low bench, which could have been sat on. Compared to the well-executed carved sculptures and pillars, this is a crude and misshapen splayed figure with minimal facial features, small drooping breasts that hang to the side of the torso, and scrawny arms and legs. Most striking, however, is the exposure of the body, the complete opening up of the naked form. Specifically, the explicit depiction of the genital region, previously unknown in the Turkish and Levantine Neolithic, is marked by an engraved hole that might be interpreted as being penetrated by a disconnected penis....Since the splayed figure is the only female portrayal from Göbekli, was on a bench that people may have sat on, and is a passively penetrated figure, one might interpret this as not being a particularly positive rendition of women and as unlikely to be associated with notions of fertility or matriarchy."[87]

You could say that. Maybe our Neolithic ancestors in the Near East could have used a "#McToo" movement.

I feel wretched. This can't be right. I bend under the crushing weight, as though the fifteen-ton monolith with the belt across the middle is coming down on me. In my distraught state, I wake up from a dream and the words come streaming through my brain. "But penises are for me to love! Not to hang over my head. Not to make me disappear!" How can I say this and be understood? Our genitals are for joining and bonding. The penis evolved to love, not to dominate.

When I look at the monolithic apparently male sculpture, it actually is very beautiful, with its long arm and fingers carved down the side and strange markings on the top cross piece. It seems to be from another world, as Schmidt pointed out many times, calling it "supernatural." There must be interpretations that do not project our current gods and gender conflict onto the past.

Around and under these giant humanoid figures (which, it should be emphasized again, do not have any genitals) are predators with their teeth showing and their penises erect, mixed in with scorpions, spiders, snakes and lizards. It is a splendid display of the natural world as experienced by people who lived close to the ground. And it's more than that.

In fact, it could have been a place where the dead were taken to leave their mortal coils and be returned as spirit. Raptors, known to be used in defleshing the dead, appear often on the monoliths and the ground around the columns was full of bones. Painted and altered skulls have also been found, indicating ritualistic use. The skulls were from people already dead.

"Images of decapitated human heads in the clutches of raptors or predators are common at Göbekli," writes young Australian archaeologist Anna Fagan in a guest commentary for the team of excavators.[88] But she said, these "themes of death and predation at Göbekli should not be perceived as destructive but rather, co-productive. Manifest is the network of relations upon which life itself depends: the cycle of death, consumption and reproduction....It was conceivably through predatory consumption of the deceased that the human soul was released, flesh transmuted into spirit matter, and vitality redistributed."

Fagan's interpretation appeals to me. I see material life as a process of continual transformation, as we and everything on Earth arises, consumes, decays and is reabsorbed back into the earth. We eat each other. A repeating cycle of creation and destruction is nature's way. That's just the way it is. Everything I have read about the sacred female in prehistory tells me that our ancestors saw this as well, except that regeneration may have been more personal to them than it is to me. I have no belief that flesh gets "transmuted into spirit matter," though part of me wishes that were true.

I'm ready to leave Göbekli Tepe behind. It has been a shock to see such dominant masculine symbols in the first temple built by humans, or rather by men. It was hard to go looking for evidence of female divinity in the Neolithic and be confronted instead with this sanctuary full of penises. It's also been difficult to square the sheer size of these monoliths with the small handheld artifacts that appear later as indicators of a belief in female divinity—even though there are thousands of them.

Is size important? I don't know. Men tend to build monuments to themselves; women not so much. Perhaps this was a male sanctuary or round house and men just like to see themselves as bigger than life.

Göbekli Tepe was covered over 10,000 years ago. No one knows why. It was built and used for less than 2,000 years and then buried for centuries until 1994 when it came to light in current times, posing more questions than it answered.

FIVE MONTHS LATER

I've solved the Rorschach!

Mock, criticize, denounce, ignore—I care not. I have found the answer to the mystery of Göbekli Tepe in a totally unexpected place—the ethnography of mother-centered cultures by Heide Göettner-Abendroth.

She claims that megalithic installations (presumably like those at Stonehenge and Göbekli Tepe) were built by matriarchal people. Moreover, there is ethnographic evidence to back up her point.

The Khasi, indigenous to the northeastern states of India such as Assam, are an extant culture whose history reaches back into the Neolithic, and they are megalith builders. Hauling in huge stones from nearby mountains, the Khasi have been witnessed setting up megalithic monuments to their ancestors—big standing stones called menhirs to represent male protectors and flat horizontal stones called dolmens to represent female ancestors.

"There is a definite arrangement for the groups of stones," writes Göettner-Abendroth. (There are) "three standing stones (menhirs) and, in front of them, a large, horizontal stone (dolmen) resting on stone supports, like a table. Sometimes the menhirs may be in groups of five, seven or more (always an odd number), all of them in a row and always with a dolmen in the front or center. The stones embody the dead ancestors for whom they were built; in this everlasting form they can forever stay among the living. This is why we sometimes see some of these stones with carved faces.

"The large, horizontal stone is the ancestress of the clan, who, according to Khasi belief, deserves to lie down and rest after all her hard work. Every dolmen is thus a female stone....Though the standing menhirs are male, they are not erect penises (as some researchers would have it) but rather embodiments of the whole men. The middle stone, which is the tallest in the row, represents the eldest brother...the watchman and protector of her eternal peace. That's why he's standing up! The other menhirs stand as other brothers or sons of the mythical ancestress."[89]

Göbekli Tepe was built 10,000 years before this modern installation by the Khasi, but similarities between the two sites are astounding. Now I understand my instinctual reaction to the beautiful, peaceable carving on the standing pillars. These are protectors, not aggressors, not conquerers or masters over nature. Along with the horizontal stones representing females, they honor the memory of their ancestors. Göbekli Tepe is a place for ancestor worship, and the skulls found there support that idea.

Female ancestors were not carved in humanoid form into the stone; they were represented by the stone itself, the bench on which food was served (there's evidence of feasting at the site). That also is characteristic of the Khasi, where the dolmen represents a female ancestor and is a place of feasting.

As for the scratched-in figure of the female at Göbekli Tepe, it is probably the first example of graffiti in the world, added after the site was built or abandoned, according to the last sentence describing the excavation site on the blog from Göbekli:

"The hitherto only known clearly female depiction is a later added graffito on a stone slab in one of the buildings of Layer II, which was most likely not an original decoration of that room." (my ital.)[90]

Now I can sleep better.

THIRTEEN

SHE SPEAKS

I am in Turkey, crossing Anatolia, the ancient land of some of the earliest human settlements. It is 2011. Less than 400 miles to the southeast, war has begun in Syria, which cancels my trip to Aleppo. My heart aches to think of the destruction being wrought in the center of this richly detailed prehistoric region. Within a circumference of just a few hundred miles, from Anatolia to the Levant, our ancestors built the first known towns and temples on Earth.

There was no chance to see Çatalhöyük, but suddenly, out of the window of the bus, a monument appeared on a flat empty plain, striking me with wonder. It was a large, standing Hittite fountain from about 1,500 BC, marked with stone pillars and figures worn down by the ages. Water still gushed from the natural spring there, but the animal forms, bulls and lions, had been melted by weather until their identities were only suggested—the lion by its wide-open mouth. Disembarking from the bus, I ran around the fountain and I saw goddesses. You couldn't mistake them, with their ample bosoms. Squat, fertile, sexual, they stood at the source of the water, evidence of the power of the divine feminine. The Hittites were a different people from those at Çatalhöyük 3,000 years earlier, yet they had the same symbols—bulls and goddesses.

The Hittites had invaded Anatolia from the steppes in centuries past and had adopted the religion that was native to the area, practiced by indigenous people called the Hattians. One of the major deities in Hatti was a sun goddess (there was also a sun god), so the sacred female had a home in Anatolia for thousands of years, and not only there, but in Mesopotamia to the east and in the Aegean to the west.

An enduring sacred complex—bulls and goddesses—was carried from Anatolia to early Mediterranean populations, to the 220 small islands known as the Cyclades, and to the larger island of Crete, where the Minoans built an amazing culture.

I was in Turkey with Janet—one of a half-dozen international trips we took in the new century—and we were on our way from Konya, in central Anatolia, to Antalya, Turkey's ancient gateway to the Mediterranean. We continued on around the southern coast of Turkey, from Antalya to Fethiye Bay where we embarked on a journey by sea to the port city of Marmaris. These coastal mountains were once occupied by the Lycian people, of whom Herodotus wrote, "They have customs that resemble no one else's. They use their mother's name instead of their father's. If one Lycian asks another from whom he is descended, he gives the name of his mother."[91]

The Lycians have a more famous claim to fame; they supposedly formed the first democracy in history and, while it's doubtful they continued a matrilineal tradition into the age of patriarchy, they may have had female leaders of the assembly—at least, by some reports.

As we hiked down the hills toward Fethiye Bay, I glimpsed through the trees the incredible blue-green, transparent water of the Turquoise Coast below. For thousands of years, during the Bronze Age and earlier, humans crossed these mountains, carrying their knowledge and culture from Anatolia to the wider world, most especially the tools of agriculture. I imagined them embarking to cross the Mediterranean Sea in their long rowboats, like the one I glimpsed in Istanbul at an exhibition of artifacts from the Cyclades.

It was the first exhibition of Cycladic art and artifacts ever held in Turkey. Titled "Across. The Cyclades and Western Anatolia During the 3rd Millennium BC," the exhibition demonstrated the affinity between Anatolian people and the islands of the Mediterranean, a relationship that had begun at least as early as 6,000 BCE,[92] during the Stone Age along maritime routes and over land.

In one display case after another, I saw female figures—small, marble cream-colored, nearly faceless figures, their arms crossed over their midsection, artifacts that support beliefs that this was a goddess culture. Although some have called them "dolls," their abstract, expressionless faces lifted up to the skies look like devotional icons.

The item that gave me goosebumps, however, was the Cycladic boat. At forty-six feet, it stood alone in a museum hall, the walls of which had to be removed to get it in. With no nails and no joints, it was a work of art, like those that carried people from the Cycladic archipelago in the Aegean to Crete, to the Turkish coasts and back. The maritime trade route across these distances would include the time Çatalhöyük was flourishing.

The exhibition reflected the Bronze Age, which (depending on which region of the old world we are talking about) began about 5,000 years ago. "Third Millennium BC": the words have a wonderful sound to them, reflective of the sophisticated cultures that flourished throughout the Near East, Egypt, southeastern Europe and the Mediterranean—creating a web of trading and cultural exchange that lasted almost 2,000 years. All of these cultures worshipped a goddess of one sort or another, and while they also left evidence of gods, the presence of a sacred female was an outstanding feature of Bronze Age civilization.

BRONZE AGE GODDESSES

Inanna was not alone among Bronze Age goddesses for inspiring terror. A thousand years later, in Egypt, a ferocious goddess appears along the Nile River (approx. 1,400 BCE). Her name is Sekhmet, which meant "power," and she wore the head of a lioness. In a story from that era, which was contemporaneous with Minoan culture, Sekhmet is called upon to punish humankind for their disdainful attitude toward the gods. She enters the field of battle and begins tearing humans limb from limb, drinking their blood in the process. She drinks enough to enter a frenzy and can't be stopped. On the verge of annihilating the human race, Sekhmet is so ferocious that even the gods can't stop her until they mix blood with alcohol or plant medicines (depending on which version you read) and spread it over the ground. Sekhmet drinks that down too and, drunk, she loses consciousness. When she awakes, she no longer has a lust for blood. Tamed (for the moment), Sekhmet has time to exercise her other powers, particularly those of healing, or, as in the manifestation of Hathor, to be the goddess of love, gaiety, sex and childbirth.

As the patron of healers and physicians, Sekhmet also joined the powers of light and dark, being both a creative and a destructive force—the Lady of Life and the Lady of Terror both. The all-encompassing range of Bronze Age goddesses often included a concern with justice, so that destructiveness could be directed against evil and was not completely arbitrary. Such was the case with Sekhmet and with the much later manifestation of a terrifying goddess, Kali.

Inanna (also called Ishtar, Isis, Asherah) and Sekhmet came on the scene 2,000-3,000 years before the Hindu goddess Kali (sixth century AD), but they were like her and it's probable that Kali's complex joining of love and wrath derives from Mesopotamian religion. Kali may be the last surviving symbol of the incredible range of Bronze Age goddesses.

The story of this kind of sacred female, soon destroyed by Abrahamic religions, thrills me because it opens the door to full and equal exercise of power by women. There is a place for ferocity, a place for wildness, a place for lust. We are not just maternal and caring; we can use power to reorient humankind. I don't particularly want to drink blood, but I do feel a strong urge to defy death and smash those who cause pain. I see why men fear the power of this ancient goddess. There is something primal, even atavistic, about the power she represented. It cannot be defeated. Yet, that same power had a regenerative, positive side as well—all held within the same container. That is, in fact, the true identity of a Goddess of Nature.

THE GARDEN OF EDEN

Sometime around 1,500 BCE, Abraham would be born in the city of Ur, where Enheduanna had written her poetry. He would become the founder of the three great patriarchal religions: Judaism, Christianity and Islam. War, statehood and the invention of writing came together in massive social change under the banner of kings, armies and an all-male God. It was a revolutionary time to rival anything we have seen in human history.

The vivid story told by Merlin Stone in *When God Was a Woman* about the Garden of Eden recounts the systematic way in which the new Hebrew religion displaced the symbols of the goddess, turning the snake into an agent of evil and placing the curse of original sin upon women. Stone also recounts widespread massacres of goddess-worshipping populations that occurred during this period.

Inanna would not have tolerated anything like a Garden of Eden, demolishing the idyllic dream created by the sacred mountain, Ebih, as inconsistent with the natural world. The biblical God reinstated the idyll, only to make women responsible for its loss and then to give men control over both women and nature. In this way, the evil we know in the world was pushed into the subconscious, where it could bubble as the dark feminine, unexamined by good men.

THE FIRST DARK AGE

This entire interconnected civilization collapsed about 3,100 years ago (approx. 1,200 BCE) in a cataclysm that included earthquake, volcanic eruption, drought, famine and war/invasion, ushering in the world's first Dark Ages. With that collapse,

primary goddess worship also was lost, to be resurrected in minimized, fractured form by the classical Greeks several hundred
years later.

There is much to say about Bronze Age goddesses, particularly that of the Minoan civilization on the island of Crete. It is
enormously difficult to understand a religion without the written
word; the Minoans left a minimal script called Linear A, which
has not been and probably cannot be translated because there isn't
enough of it. In spite of the difficulties, however, classical scholar
Nanno Marinatos, of the University of Illinois in Chicago, has
produced a brilliant reading of the images these people left on
artifacts and walls. Most of what I write here about the Minoan
goddess comes from her work, *Minoan Religion: Ritual, Image,
and Symbol.*

From the many images Marinatos scrutinized, she concludes
that the Minoan sacred female was unambiguously a nurturing goddess of nature, usually depicted outdoors among plants,
flowers and animals, including lions, which she often feeds. In
one scene, her costume and face

> are decorated with crocus flowers. Around her neck,
> she has a triple necklace with duck and dragon-
> fly pendants....Her attendants are a monkey and
> a griffin...The divinity thus incorporates several
> aspects of nature: aquatic and terrestrial, animals,
> insects and flowers....A most powerful image is the
> afore-mentioned Mother of the Mountains. The
> goddess stands on a mountaintop, with her arm out-
> stretched in a gesture of command, displaying her
> staff of authority. She is flanked by lions.[93]

Other sources have noted mountaintop sanctuaries where
Minoans worshipped a goddess associated with the sun.
Marinatos does not mention a solar deity but clearly the goddess
she describes was linked to the seasons and may have included

sun worship. Other people of the Bronze Age, those in Anatolia and Egypt, also had female solar deities, so this appearance of the goddess was widespread in the interconnected Mediterranean world long before the sun god Ra appeared in Egypt in what has been called the first monotheistic religion.

The Minoan goddess, however, stands out strongly during this era because she was not a warrior. Crete's peaceful orientation at this time was evident in its lack of fortifications, as well as in its nature divinities. One manifestation of the goddess was as a bird—a human with a bird head—much like those Gimbutas wrote about in Eastern Europe.

And like many, if not most, egalitarian societies, both genders had divine form, so the Minoans had gods as well. Less central than the female divinity, the gods were also associated with nature, not with war. They appeared on artifacts, as young and robust, somewhat like hunters. Where the goddess might be seen feeding animals, the gods were displayed as controlling them. In one instance, lions were depicted as honoring the god. In another case, a god stood in command, not on a mountain, but over a city.

Minoan culture—which collapsed along with other Bronze Age civilizations more than 3,000 years ago—provides what seems to be the last glimpse of a benevolent nature goddess, a deity who held central place in a pantheon of gods. It's been a pleasure to make her acquaintance, which happened one day in a particularly vivid way.

I woke that morning with the familiar sense of discouragement, anticipating having to deal again with the long-standing deconstruction of goddess worship by contemporary archaeologists. It had been so difficult to plow through the academic obfuscation, paper by paper, endlessly searching the Internet for evidence that survived the flood. And there it was—a TED lecture by Gareth Owens, linguist and archaeologist at the Crete Educational Technological Institute, who, with Oxford linguist John Coleman, had made progress in understanding the writing on a Minoan disk. The two had not actually translated the writing, except for three critical words referring to "Goddess." But they could sound out the syllables and employed a woman to read them.

The woman's voice read from the 3,700-year-old Phaistos disk, discovered in a palace that had possibly been the site of religious worship. When I heard that voice from the past, I was struck by wonder. I could not understand the words, but the music of the hymn soothed me, and I felt a strange sense of reverence.

For the first time in my life, I heard an actual prayer to the goddess from the ancients.[94]

Apparently, the disk, which had been baked for posterity, recorded a hymn to the goddess worshipped by these people in the second millennium before Christ. The pictorial signs they used could be transformed into syllables of which three were understood:

IQE: Mother goddess
IQEKURJA: Pregnant mother goddess
IQEPAJE: Shining mother goddess

Owens believes that one side of the disk is dedicated to the pregnant mother goddess and the other to Astarte, who had become a Minoan goddess through cultural transmission from ancient Mesopotamia. She then went on to became Venus or Aphrodite in the Greek pantheon, he said.

Of course, there is challenge to Owens's work as to all claims of goddess worship, but my journey is over. I accept this. I heard the voice. It's even better that I cannot understand it because the mystery that remains is important. Words limit and delimit a sense of reverence. It's enough to know that once upon a time, people imagined the powers of the universe in the form of a female, whom they called "Queen of Heaven."

EPILOGUE

THE PULSE OF EVERYTHING

A few weeks after my mother's death in 2010, as I was hiking through the forest on Mt. Tamalpais near San Francisco, I glanced down at my feet and saw a beautiful twig covered in leafy, blue-green lichen. My whole being was seized by the notion that I was looking at my mother and I knelt down and picked it up, suddenly seeing spirit everywhere—in the trees, the air, the moss. It was Mother Nature and I realized at that moment what it must have been like for our long distant ancestors in the Neolithic to feel reverence in the natural environment. It has taken many years to learn such reverence for myself, my body, my mother and the natural world that brings us into life.

THE MYSTERY

How do I write about divinity? What is a divine thing anyway? The notion of an actual goddess is unacceptable to my twenty-first century, scientifically trained mind. Yet, I need this presence in my consciousness. I need her strength, her aliveness. I need to know that I am connected to something greater than my little ego. I don't have to believe to get the benefit of knowing this deity. She can, and does, exist as a kind of archetype that helps give me strength and perspective.

As I've written this book, I have hewed as closely as I could to the existing evidence of belief in an ancient goddess. I am committed to verifiable information and authoritative references. It's been a bit hard at times because of the enduring and recurring tendency to write women's contributions out of the male-dominated canon. But now, I want to return to my own emotional and spiritual development.

I am a practitioner of Zen Buddhism. We are not theists; there is no anthropomorphic god. I struggle to comprehend the "Big Self"—the part of my mind that is not involved with ego (Small Self) but relates to a larger universe of being. It is a state of awareness, without God but with a sense of connection to all things—no separation. Many Zen writings describe this kind of belief system, but in my humble opinion, they are extremely difficult to comprehend, written as they are, in an original language—Japanese—that is based on Chinese, and before that, Sanskrit, and before that a dead language, Pali, which few people can read. Moreover, Zen writers often aim at obfuscation since they want to disrupt the rational brain, hoping to produce an awareness that moves beyond words and intellectual description. Indeed, it has done that for me over the past twenty years of meditation and practice.

I know that everything changes; that nothing is fixed. I know that I have no essential nature, that I change with every relationship and every new environment. Yet, I am me, an awareness that stretches into the past, stitching together the story of my mind. This "self" is integral and central and while it has many parts, it feels as permanent as any other thing in life, which is to say, it also will pass into transformation when the time comes. But the "me" is here now and it is connected. So, I taste the universe once in a while. I lie in the web of interconnections that make up the world of things. In those moments, I pass beyond the intellect into immediate experience. And it feels good.

I'm not sure what all this means for my thesis in this memoir. But somehow, it is connected with the reality of the natural world, which is so beautiful, so mysterious and so damn tricky. You can't count on anything staying around. It comes and goes and all you can do is move with the waves, knowing that another one will come to lift you up temporarily or throw you helplessly into a whirl of white water.

This isn't a spiritual belief to sooth the soul. It's a means of touching the way things really are in a constantly changing world. You can't hang on to anything.

Yet we live, we breathe. We wake up every morning and do our business. Something is solid; I should say we want to *believe* something is solid because to think otherwise is to be looking out all the time for disruptive change. Knowing that nothing is permanent, the everyday becomes precious to me. I live on the edge. And I seek tranquility. That's why I meditate.

I don't see the natural world as a goddess or any other kind of deity (at least not with my rational mind). I'd like to think there is some pattern to reality that sustains us, some overall consciousness that knows when we act wisely and furthers our action in the world, but I'm a doubter and don't believe in such a force. I think reality is neutral, arbitrary, changeable, without love or care for individual pieces of material life, such as me. This causes me more than a little existential angst, along with millions of other so-called "secular humanists."

Our ancestors from the deep past probably saw divine nature all around them. Maybe they heard plants and nonhuman animals speak. The natural world had purpose, intention, benevolence or malevolence. Seeing deities in the material world instead of molecules and atoms, they appealed to goddesses and gods for release from their suffering. Whether that appeal ever had consequences for them, no one can say, but our own suffering, unmitigated by divine help, tells us that prayers to god/desses does no good—though the prayer itself may help the soul of a believer.

Yet there is a mystery. We have this DNA that arose with the plants and animals of the deep past. Most of our genetic material we share with other living things. The bonding that makes cells stick together comes to us as love. We feel the attraction, the chemistry and so we can say that love holds everything together, that our experience with some sort of transcendental power is mediated through chemicals in our bodies and brains that speak in terms of love. It's a short hop from this more or less logical view of reality to a belief in Gaia, the Goddess of Nature, to a belief that the whole world is a single living organism.

I have difficulty making that step. Is the universe conscious? How would I ever know? All I can use as information are the mystical experiences that arise in my completely sober mind from time to time. They are rare and all the more memorable because of it.

A bush spoke to me once, just a few years ago, in a grove of glorious Sequoia trees in the Sierra Nevada mountains. It was spring. I was walking along going nowhere, with sun filtering through the enormous redwoods, when I stopped and touched a bush. With no warning, love struck like a sword, along with the name of my former partner. The feeling was so powerful, it almost bent me over and I was sure that something had been transmitted to me from that bush—though the experience was completely in my own mind; I did not actually "hear" the bush speak. I stood for long moments listening to wind ruffle the leaves of a nearby aspen and knew that I had dropped through the logical parts of my brain into circuits that could experience some other reality. There was love and it was universal, as well as particular.

Why did the bush speak to me at that time, in that place? Could it have been the spring, the fresh, growing buds on the bush that connected to the nerve endings in my fingers?

Here's another mystery.

Coral, lying beneath the ocean waves, will release a blizzard of eggs and sperm once a year in a reproductive frenzy that occurs a few days after a full moon. Truly. The coral have no eyes, yet these tiny creatures react to the light in a wave that flashes across the reef, releasing billions of gametes that float to the surface and combine to create new life. It all happens during a waning full moon when ocean temperatures have reached a certain level. Diving in the midst of this sexual release is like swimming through a "snowstorm," according to people who have witnessed the festival.

The coral, it seems, possess a primitive photoreceptor gene that allows them to "see" the moonlight in the water. Undoubtedly, humans also react more than we realize to changes of light, seasons and other natural cycles that permeate our bodies and move our emotions, but are only dimly, if at all, acknowledged by our logical brains.

And did you know that the Earth has a pulse, which vibrates at about the same rate as the beating of your heart? University of Utah geologists used seismometers to measure the movement of a tall rock formation in Utah called Castleton Tower and published its movements as audible sound.[95]

I heard the pulse at a Bioneers Conference in 2019 where conservationist Terry Tempest Williams pled for us to save the Earth and ourselves. My heart lifted in amazement as I sat in an audience of several thousand people and listened. Williams stood in silence at the podium for long moments as she broadcast the vibrations. Over our heads and throughout the auditorium we heard the Earth's heartbeat.

"Castle Rock is alive," said Williams. The Earth has a pulse, as do we. There is no separation."

Here's another thing to ponder: there are about 1,000 known plants in the world that when ingested can cause various kinds of religious experience. Today, we call them "entheogens" (capable of causing a nonordinary spiritual state of mind). In the 1960s, they were named "psychedelics." These plants grow naturally all over the globe and, according to the botanical book *Plants of the Gods*, indigenous people have used these plants for thousands of years.[96]

I often read the book when I awake at three o'clock in the morning and can't sleep. Its stories of indigenous rituals fascinate me and its botanical descriptions make me drowsy. I go back to sleep with a good dose of spiritual slumber. A common story about the early Hindu god, Soma, is that the deity was actually a hallucinogenic mushroom named *Amanita muscaria*, leading to speculation that early mysticism—the foundations of religion in western human society—were produced by using plant hallucinogens. An interesting thought.

As our world strives to regain equality between men and women in terms of power and authority, it comes with a return of Gaia energy. We've suffered enough from the restricted spheres of patriarchy, perpetuated by beliefs in one male God, who lives in the sky separated from nature. The female deity is embodied, deeply connected with Earth and the natural world. As the gender that grows and nurtures new life, women have mental and physical experiences that are unique to them. The feminine half of humanity needs its sacred mirror now as never before.

I am fortunate that I have tasted Gaia energy in profound ways, with the help of medicines such as Ecstasy (MDMA) and psilocybin. One day in 2013, in my first experience with the anti-traumatic medicine MDMA, I began to moan as I experienced my old trauma with death at the age of thirteen. At one point, after about an hour lying on the couch moaning, I suddenly said out loud, "I am going to die." My guide jumped up from the couch where she was working on her email while listening for my reassuring moans.

"You mean now?" she asked quickly. I said, "No, but eventually." She answered more quietly, "We all are going to die." I went back into the darkness behind the mask that covered my eyes.

The timbre of the moans became lower. I felt myself as Earth, Earth moaning, Earth in pain. More time passed. The moans became rhythmic as if I were a whale communicating in the deep. It was a wondrous sound to me—the sound of the deep, the sound of Earth talking, the sound of mystery. This was Gaia, the Earth goddess.

The natural world moves in so many ways, so far beyond our ken. I would not even want to know the details because such answers would come to us in scientific terms stripped of beauty and mystery. I would rather feel myself drawn inexorably outdoors by the light of a full moon, transported for a moment to god knows where. I stop. I stare upward. I am caught. I feel reverence.

That is enough.

GLOSSARY

FOUR CRITICAL DEFINITIONS

Deep confusion over four terms — male dominance, patriarchy, matriarchy and egalitarian — has prevented wide understanding of equality in human culture for many generations. These four words and their underlying concepts have generated passionate academic argument; careers have been won and lost over them. Here I define my use of the words and the sources I have used.

Male Dominance — a cultural pattern with a gender hierarchy in which women hold little or no economic power and are vulnerable to physical abuse by men. This pattern has existed in most if not all parts of the world for as long as anthropologists have kept records. It stems from environmental or cultural stress on a group, which then organizes to create a masculine ethos in men who are conditioned to kill and be killed. The pattern also dominates in pastoral, herding cultures where men supply most of the food. Main source of information: the cross-cultural studies of Peggy Reeves Sanday.

Patriarchy — a stratified formalized hierarchy that affects both genders and is strongly male dominant. It arose with the development of kings, states and armies in about the 4th millennium BCE in Mesopotamia (the antecedent of Western culture). Patriarchy follows the Agricultural Revolution and coincides with early imperialism, invasion, and the development of writing. Both patriarchy and male dominance are marked in the spiritual realm by all-male gods. But only patriarchy carries the sheen of "civilization." Many sources of information, including *The Creation of Patriarchy*, by Gerda Lerner.

Matriarchy — a cultural pattern in which women hold economic power and most often pass the inheritance of land through the maternal line. Such cultures are not based on a gender hierarchy; men and women are equally valuable and, although women retain the land and distribute the culture's food and other resources, they do not dominate men nor hold all the political power. Governance is done by consensus. Other descriptors of this system include "matrifocal," "matristic," "mother-centered." Main source of information: *Matriarchal Societies: Studies on Indigenous Cultures Across the Globe*, by Heide Goettner-Abendroth.

Egalitarian —a cultural pattern indistinguishable from "matriarchy," as defined above.
I originally used the term "matriarchal" for these gender-equal societies, but changed to "egalitarian" mid-way through the writing to remove the layers of misunderstanding and academic argument that interfere with public awareness of the nature of women's power and authority. There is no such thing as "mother's rule," as a companion piece to "father's rule." Egalitarian culture is the true opposite of patriarchy.

ENDNOTES

1   Patricia McBroom, *Behavioral Genetics,* National Institute of Mental Health, 1980.

2   Richard B. Lee, Irven DeVore, *Man the Hunter* (Chicago: Aldine Pub., 1968).

3   Frances Dahlberg, ed. *Woman the Gatherer* (New Haven: Yale University Press, 1981).

4   To give credit, Lévi-Strauss's theory that culture is built on certain enduring structural qualities of human society rather than on the genes of individuals seems entirely appropriate. Women, because they give birth, for instance, are not good candidates for becoming warriors, while men can be put in harm's way to protect the tribe. It takes ten women, but only one man, to produce ten children. This built-in gender disparity structures culture in certain ways when the need arises. In the case of bride exchange, the need is for tribes to build alliances with each other by exchanging gifts—all fine and good, except that in this case, women become chattel, just another lemon grove to be exchanged.

5   Barbara B. Smuts, *Sex and Friendship in Baboons* (New Brunswick, NJ: Aldine Transactions, 1985).

6   Merlin Stone, *When God was a Woman* (Boston: Mariner Books, 1978).

7   Anne Barstow, "The Uses of Archaeology for Women's History: James Mellaart's Work on the Neolithic Goddess at Çatal Hüyük," *Feminist Studies* 4, no. 3 (October 1978): 7-17.

8   James Mellaart, "Çatal-Hüyük. A Neolithic Town in Anatolia," Internet Archive, 107-8.

9   Barstow, Ibid, 7-18.

10   Marija Gimbutas, *The Language of the Goddess*, (New York: Thames & Hudson, Inc., 2001) 321.

11   Ibid, xix.

12   Peggy Reeves Sanday, *Female Power and Male Dominance*, (New York: Cambridge University Press, 1981) 169.

13   Ibid, 168.

14   Ibid, 182.

15   Ibid, 187-8.

16   Ibid, 33.

17   Ibid, 35.

18   Ibid, 211.

19   Deborah S. Rogers, Omkar Deshpande, Marcus W. Feldman, "The Spread of Inequality," *PLOS ONE* 6, no. 9: e24683.

20   Alice Schlegel, Herbert Barry, III, "Pain, Fear and Circumcision in Boys, Adolescent Initiation Ceremonies," C*ross-Cultural Research*, 51, no. 5 (January 7, 2017): 435-463.

21   Gregory Bateson, *Naven*, (Stanford: Stanford University Press, 1958).

22 Ibid, 130.

23 Ibid, 131.

24 Ibid, 131.

25 Carol R. Ember, Melvin Ember, "Explaining Male Initiation Ceremonies: New Cross-Cultural Tests," *Journal of Cross-Cultural Psychology* 41, no. 4 (July 20, 2010): 605-616.

26 Peggy Orenstein, *Boys & Sex*, (New York: Harper Collins, 2020).

27 Andrew Reiner, "Teaching Men to be Emotionally Honest," *The New York Times*, April 4, 2016.

28 Salvatore DeGennaro, "Why Leftists Hate Masculinity," *American Thinker*, January 17, 2018.

29 David French, "Trump's Counterfeit Masculinity," *National Review*, April 18, 2016.

30 Christopher Jones and Linton Satterthwaite, Jr., *The Monuments and Inscriptions of Tikal—The Carved Monuments: Tikal Report 33A*, (Philadelphia: Uni. of Penn. Press).

31 Coe finally did publish in 1990 a six-volume stratigraphic description of the architecture of central Tikal, a "stunning and dramatic achievement," that left the reviewer, William Fash, "awestruck" at the quality of the drawings, maps and detailed sections. But Fash added, "the greatest disappointment to this reader was that after all that work, after over three decades of patient, laborious and admirable effort, Coe only occasionally allowed himself and the reader the luxury of seeing in print his interpretations of the North Acropolis and Great Plaza developments in terms other than their own "stratigraphic

milieux"…[Coe failed to] illuminate the very questions that
generated this research in the first place: the nature of the rise,
development and fall of lowland Maya civilization." William L.
Fash, "Reflections on a Monument to a Monument: A Review of
Tikal Report 14," *American Anthropologist* 94 (1992): 400-5.

32   Dava Sobel, "Alcohol Plagues Eskimos," *The New York Times,*
     January 22, 1980.

33   Patricia McBroom, "Dark Nights of the Soul Under the Midnight
     Sun," *Today Magazine, Philadelphia Inquirer,* April 27, 1980.

34   Patricia McBroom, *The Third Sex: The New Professional Woman,*
     (New York: William Morrow and Company, 1986).

35   Arlie Russell Hochschild, "The Totaled Woman," *The New York
     Times,* May 11, 1986.

36   Diane Wolkstein and Samuel Noah Kramer, *Inanna, Queen of
     Heaven and Earth,* (New York: Harper & Row, 1983) 12.

37   Ibid, 43.

38   Betty De Shong Meador, *Inanna, Lady of Largest Heart,* (Austin:
     Uni. of Texas Press, 2000).

39   Ibid, 159.

40   Wolkstein and Kramer, xix.

41   Meador, 134.

42   Ibid, 151.

43 Judy Grahn, "Ecology of the Erotic in a Myth of Inanna," *International Journal of Transpersonal Studies*, 29, no. 2 (2010): 58-67.

44 Meador, 17.

45 Ibid, 152.

46 Meador, 100.

47 Ibid, 138.

48 Rick Fields, "The Very Short Sutra on the Meeting of the Buddha and the Goddess," from *Dharma Gaia: A Harvest of Essays in Buddhism and Ecology*, (Berkeley: Parallax Press, 1990) 3.

49 Kathryn McCamant and Charles Durrett, "*Cohousing: A Contemporary Approach to Housing Ourselves*, (Berkeley: Ten Speed Press, 1988).

50 Eleanor Leacock, "Gender in Egalitarian Societies," from *Becoming Visible: Women in European History, 2nd ed.,* ed. Renate Bridenthal and Claudia Koonz (Boston: Houghton Mifflin Co., 1987).

51 M. Dyble, et al, "Sex equality can explain the unique social structure of hunter-gatherer bands," *Science*, 348, no. 6236 (May 15, 2015): 796-798. Anthropologists in London wrote that early hunters and gatherers profited from gender equality because the influence of women led them to team up with unrelated individuals. People did not stick to their kin. Instead, they moved around, back and forth between families of the mother and father, with the result that many unrelated individuals would end up living together. In the African Congo, where this study was done, unrelated and distant relatives made up about 50 percent of these

small bands. "Co-residence with unrelated individuals set the selective environment for the evolution of hyper-cooperation and pro-sociality." This took place without the accumulation of wealth.

52 Ian Hodder, "Women and Men at Çatalhöyük," *Scientific American*, SA Special Editions 15, no. 1s, January 2005, 34-41.

53 Anne Barstow, "The Prehistoric Goddess," from ed. Carl Olson, *The Book of the Goddess, Past and Present*, (New York: The Crossroad Publishing Co., 1992).

54 Barbara Alice Mann, *Iroquoian Women: The Gantowisas*, (New York: Peter Lang Pub., 2000): 150-1

55 Sally Roesch Wagner, *Sisters in Spirit: Haudenosaunee (Iroquois) Influence on Early American Feminists*, (Summertown, TN: Native Voices Book Pub. Co., 2001).

56 Mann, Ibid, 38.

57 Ibid, 180.

58 Ibid, 59.

59 Yang Erche Namu and Christine Mathieu, *Leaving Mother Lake: A Girlhood at the Edge of the World*, (New York: Little, Brown and Company, 2003).

60 Ibid, 8.

61 Ibid, 17.

62 Ibid, 34.

63 Peggy Reeves Sanday, *Women at the Center: Life in a Modern Matriarchy,* (Ithaca: Cornell University Press, 2002).

64 Chandra K. Roy, "Indigenous Women: A Gender Perspective," *Aboriginal Policy Research Consortium International (APRCi)* (May 2004).

65 United Nations Permanent Forum on Indigenous Peoples, "Gender and Indigenous Peoples: Briefing Note #1," United Nations Office of the Special Adviser on Gender Issues and Advancement of Women, June 2009.

66 Heidi Göettner-Abendroth, *Matriarchal Societies: Studies on Indigenous Cultures Across the Globe* (New York: Peter Lang, Inc., 2012). Göettner-Abendroth, who originally taught philosophy at the University of Munich, abandoned what she experienced as a male-dominated academic environment and, in 1986, established the International Academy HAGIA to further the study of matriarchal cultures. She sponsored two World Congresses on Matriarchal Studies in 2003 and 2005, and in 2005 was one of 1,000 women nominated for the Nobel Peace Prize.

67 Orenstein, Ibid.

68 Rosabeth Moss Kantor, *World Class: Thriving Locally in the Global Economy,* (New York: Simon & Schuster, 1995).

69 Arlie Russell Hochschild, *Strangers in Their Own Land,* (New York: The New Press, 2016).

70 Gerda Lerner, *The Creation of Feminist Consciousness,* (New York: Oxford Uni. Press, 1993).

71 Charlene Spretnak, "Anatomy of a Backlash," *Journal of Archaeomythology* 7 (2011): 25-51.

72   Joan Marler, "The Myth of Universal Patriarchy: A Critical
     Response to Cynthia Eller's Myth of Matriarchal Prehistory,"
     Feminist Theology 14, no. 2 (January 2006): 163-187.

73   Douglass W. Bailey, "The Figurines of Old Europe," ed. D.W.
     Anthony, *The Lost World of Old Europe: The Danube Valley, 5000-
     3500 BC,* (New York: Princeton Uni. Press, 2010) 112-127.

74   Douglass W. Bailey, "Southeast European Neolithic Figurines:
     Beyond Context, Interpretation and Meaning," ed. Timothy Insoll,
     The Oxford Handbook of Prehistoric Figurines, (Oxford: Oxford Uni
     Press, 2017).

75   Richard G. Lesure, "Comparative Perspectives in the
     Interpretation of Prehistoric Figurines," *The Oxford Handbook
     of Prehistoric Figurine*s, (Oxford, Eng.: Oxford University Press,
     2017) 57.

76   Lucy Goodison and Christine Morris, *Ancient Goddesses,* (London:
     British Museum Press, 1998) 16.

77   Wolfgang Haak et al., "Massive Migration from the Steppe was
     a Source for Indo-European Languages in Europe," *Nature* 522
     (2015): 207–211.

78   Amy Goldberg, et al., "Ancient X Chromosomes Reveal
     Contrasting Sex Bias in Neolithic and Bronze Age Eurasian
     Migrations," *Proceedings of the National Academy of Sciences* 114, no.
     10 (March 7, 2017): 2657-2662.

79   Iosif Lazaridis, et al., "Genetic Origins of the Minoans and
     Mycenaeans," *Nature* 548 (2017): 214-218.

80   Colin Renfrew, "Marija Rediva and Indo-European Origins," The Oriental Institute, March 14, 2018, lecture on YoutTube video, Mar 14, 2018.

81   Carol P. Christ, "Marija Gimbutas Triumphant: Colin Renfrew Concedes," *Feminism and Religion* (blog), December 11, 2017.

82   Göbekli Tepe research staff, "The Site," *The Tepe Telegrams* (blog), 2020.

83   M.B. Sweatman, "Decoding Göbekli Tepe with Archaeoastronomy: What Does the Fox Say?", *Mediterranean Archaeology and Archaeometry,* 17, no. 1 (January 2017): 233-250.

84   Klaus Schmidt, 2nd lecturer, *First International Symposium on Göbeklitepe,* Sanliurfa, Turkey, October 6, 2012.

85   "Göbekli Tepe, Angels N Demons," National Geographic documentary, April 10, 2014, YouTube video.

86   C. Brian Rose, "New Discoveries in Ancient Turkey," Penn Museum lectures, November 19, 2016.

87   Lynn Meskill and Ian Hodder, "A Curious and Sometimes Trifle Macabre Artistry," *Current Anthropology* 52, no. 2 (April 2011): 235-263.

88   Anna Fagan, "Hungry Architecture, a Guest Contribution by Dr. Anna Fagan," *The Tepe Telegrams* (blog), December 18, 2017.

89   Göettner-Abendroth, "Matriarchy in Northeast India," Ch. 2: 45-68.

90   "The Site," *The Tepe Telegrams* (blog)

91 Herodotus (translated by G. C. Macaulay) *The Histories*. (Spark Educational Publishing, 2004).

92 B. Horejs, et al., "The Aegean in the Early 7th Millennium BC: Maritime Networks and Colonization," *Journal of World Prehistory* 28 (December 10, 2015): 289-330.

93 Nanno Marinatos, *Minoan Religion: Ritual, Image, and Symbol*, (Columbia, SC: Uni. of So. Carolina Press, 1993) 151.

94 Gareth Owens, "Decrypting the Phaistos Disk: Gareth Owens at TED," February 2014, YouTube video, May 23, 2014.

95 JoAnna Klein, "Taking the Pulse of a Sandstone Tower in Utah," *The New York Times,* Sept. 9, 2019.

96 Richard Evans Schultes, Albert Hofmann and Christian Ratsch, *Plants of the Gods: Their Sacred, Healing and Hallucinogenic Powers,* (Lucerne, Switz.: Healing Arts Press, 1992).

Patricia McBroom is an anthropologist, science journalist and professor of women's studies. Her 1985 book on women adapting to professional roles on Wall Street, *The Third Sex*, was described in a *New York Times* review as "a brave and stunningly intuitive journey." A former science writer at the *Philadelphia Inquirer*, McBroom earned her degree in anthropology at the University of Pennsylvania and in 1980 published a book on the genetics of behavior. She taught at Rutgers University, Mills College and the University of California at Berkeley. Her memoir challenges male-biased academic narratives of human culture and evolution with evidence of female authority in ancient and modern egalitarian societies.

ABOUT GREEN FIRE PRESS

Green Fire Press is an independent publishing company dedicated to supporting authors in producing and distributing high-quality books in fiction or non-fiction, poetry or prose. Find out more at **Greenfirepress.com**.

Other Green Fire Press titles you may also enjoy:

A Short Course In Happiness After Loss, by Maria Sirois, PsyD.

A lyrical gem of a book, combining positive psychology with the wisdom necessary to thrive when facing life's harshest moments, rising through pain into a steady, resilient and open heart.

Nature, Culture, and the Sacred: A Woman Listens For Leadership, by Nina Simons

Bioneers co-founder Nina Simons offers inspiration for anyone who aspires to grow into their own unique form of leadership with resilience and joy. Winner of the 2018 Nautilus Gold Award.

What I Forgot…and Why I Remembered: A Journey to Environmental Awareness and Activism Through Purposeful Memoir, by Jennifer Browdy, PhD.

"Inspires us to see how we can reclaim our lives for the sake of life on Earth" —Joanna Macy.

Finalist for the 2018 International Book Award.

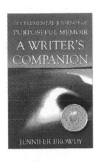

The Elemental Journey of Purposeful Memoir: A Writer's Companion, by Jennifer Browdy, PhD.

Month-by-month guidance for memoir writers.

Winner of the 2017 Nautilus Silver Award.

Writing Fire: Celebrating the Power of Women's Words, edited by Jennifer Browdy, Jana Laiz and Sahra Bateson Brubeck.

More than 75 passionate women writers share their voices and visions in this powerful anthology.

Wisdom Lessons: Spirited Guidance from an Ojibwe Great-Grandmother, by Mary Lyons

The culmination of a lifetime steeped in Indigenous spiritual traditions, Grandmother Mary offers invaluable lessons for anyone interested in living in alignment with their higher self.

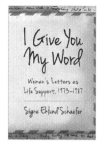

I Give You My Word: Women's Letters as Life Support, 1973–1987, by Signe Eklund Schaefer

A forgotten box of letters in a dark attic corner, messages from women friends written decades ago. An intimate record of a time of great transition in how women experienced their daily lives and imagined their future.

Dancing Full Tilt in the Light: Love, Loss & Finding Home, by Naomi Pevsner

A successful Dallas jewelry designer, Naomi had the perfect life—until the deaths of her parents send her into a place so dark, even the diamonds lose their shine. Laugh and cry with Naomi as she moves through grief into healing, sharing important life lessons for us all.

Made in the USA
Middletown, DE
23 September 2020